CW00736085
EX LIBRIS

A SUSSEX GUIDE

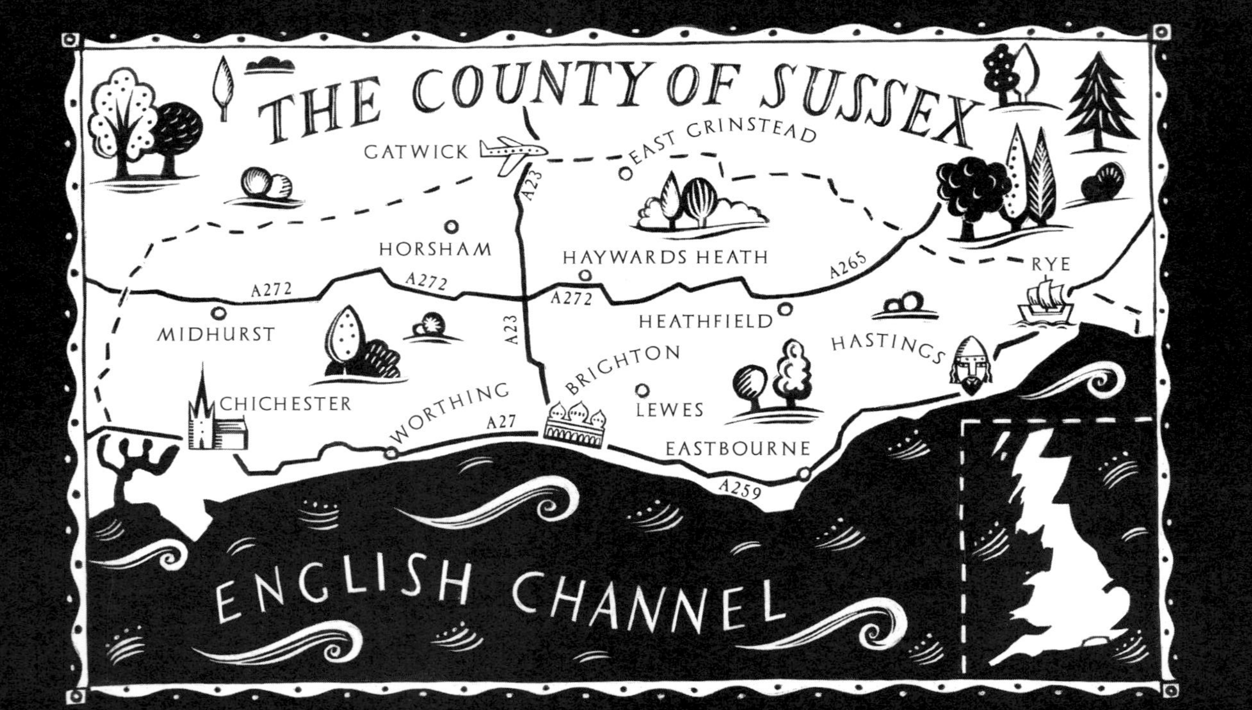
THE COUNTY OF SUSSEX
GATWICK
EAST GRINSTEAD
A23
HORSHAM
HAYWARDS HEATH
A265
RYE
A272
A272
A272
MIDHURST
HEATHFIELD
A23
HASTINGS
BRIGHTON
CHICHESTER
WORTHING
LEWES
A27
EASTBOURNE
A259
ENGLISH CHANNEL

A SUSSEX MISCELLANY

SOPHIE COLLINS

Embellished with a
SPLENDID ASSORTMENT *of*
ILLUSTRATIONS & ENGRAVINGS

SNAKE RIVER PRESS

SNAKE RIVER PRESS

Book No 9

Books about Sussex for the enthusiast

Published in 2007 by
SNAKE RIVER PRESS
South Downs Way, Alfriston, Sussex BN26 5XW
www.snakeriverpress.co.uk

ISBN 978-1-906022-08-2

This book was conceived, designed and produced by
SNAKE RIVER PRESS

ART DIRECTOR & PUBLISHER *Peter Bridgewater*
EDITORIAL DIRECTOR *Viv Croot*
EDITOR *Robert Yarham*
PAGE MAKEUP *Richard Constable & Chris Morris*
CONSULTANT *Lorraine Harrison*

This book is typeset in Perpetua & Gill Sans,
two fonts designed by Eric Gill

Printed and bound in China

DEDICATION

For Ted, who won't be druv

CONTENTS

INTRODUCTION
6

CHAPTER ONE
SUSSEX LANDSCAPES
9

CHAPTER TWO
MYTHICAL SUSSEX
25

CHAPTER THREE
HISTORICAL SUSSEX
41

CHAPTER FOUR
SUSSEX SUSTENANCE
57

CHAPTER FIVE
SUSSEX PASTIMES
73

FURTHER READING
& INDEX
91

INTRODUCTION

'The Sussex lanes were very lovely in the autumn... spendthrift gold and glory of the year-end...earth scents and the sky winds and all the magic of the countryside which is ordained for the healing of the soul'

MONICA BALDWIN, AUTHOR, NUN, & NIECE OF STANLEY BALDWIN

Putting together a miscellany starts off as a simple selection process and ends up as a treasure hunt. You begin with a clear idea of some foundation pieces that you want to include, and a less clear one of the sort of thing that is likely to be added to them. With these in mind, an orderly topic list is drawn up and work begins. And then the surprises start to emerge, and the jigsaw assembles itself, gradually revealing, piece by piece, a very different picture from the one you originally expected.

What picture would you put on a jigsaw puzzle of Sussex if you saw it in your mind's eye? What's the first thing you think of? William of Normandy, crunching up the beach at Pevensey? The Bloomsbury Group escaping from the intellectual rigours of London to their country retreat at Charleston? Perhaps the Prince Regent, proudly turning a simple farmhouse into the mad folly that can still be visited on the front at Brighton, comes to mind? Or Kipling's 'blunt, bow-headed, whale-backed Downs' that run cross-country like a crooked spine, giving Sussex its most characteristic and recognisable feature? The list can go on, and each and every picture is a valid aspect of this multi-faceted county.

West and East, its charms are exceptionally various. They are not in the main dramatic but nor are they particularly gentle. The riot of nature described by Monica Baldwin is accurate – there's nothing more bucolic than a Sussex autumn or, equally, than a late Sussex spring. (Monica Baldwin emerged in 1942 from a closed order of nuns after 28 years – on her re-emergence into a world changed beyond measure things tended to strike her especially strongly, and her writing reflects this impact.) If you spend any time in Sussex, you become aware of the bones under the skin: it can look soft, but it doesn't have the sheer prettiness of, say, the Cotswolds, nor is it as openly muscular as Cornwall or Yorkshire.

What it offers in its landscape and its atmosphere is constant changes of mood. And the people and artefacts set down in this landscape are just as varied.

Like any other southern county, by the late twentieth century Sussex had met with a new invasion – one of people. The English, from being proud of staying put where their parents bore them, have become much more mobile over the last hundred years and it's less easy than it was to pick out the famously trenchant Sussex character in its population. Here and there one comes across an echo, like the old lady in a ward in Worthing hospital in the mid-1990s, herself a native of Worthing, heard complaining bitterly to her son that 'they' had put her next to a stranger 'a Horsham woman' – to her mind, a threateningly foreign influence – but in the main one has to turn back to books and other records to catch the authentic voice of old Sussex: humorous, obstinate, parochial and fiercely independent. Luckily there is no shortage of sources to attest to these qualities, from Daniel Defoe, traipsing through Sussex in the eighteenth century and bitterly bemoaning the state of the roads, to the Reverend William Parish at the end of the nineteenth, who was so enchanted by the very particular quality of the Sussex character and the way in which it was expressed through its speech that he compiled a dictionary of the Sussex dialect that is just as absorbing for its anecdotal value as it is for its designated use.

All these elements – country, history, language, character, folklore and myth – appear here and there in *A Sussex Miscellany*. There may be things that the aficionado of Sussex lore already knows here – but hopefully there will also be some they will not. Someone who has read about the fraud of Piltdown Man may not, for example, be aware of its ornithological equivalent, the case of the Sussex Rarities; someone who knows a little of Sussex's famous reputation as a hotbed of alternative beliefs and of witchcraft may not know about the major spell cast in the 1940s to keep Britain safe from Hitler by calling up a Cone of Power. And all go to shape the impression that, as Flora Poste, Stella Gibbons' heroine in *Cold Comfort Farm*, once mused, 'Sussex, when all was said and done, was not quite like other counties...'

CHAPTER ONE

SUSSEX LANDSCAPES

The Sussex landscape has earned many admirers over the centuries – often those who, previous to encountering it, thought themselves wedded to other lands or counties. Kipling, for example, apparently believed that he would not be able to write about anywhere else as atmospherically as his beloved India, but on moving to Sussex he gradually felt himself putting down roots there and came to love it best of all. Equally, Richard Jefferies was best known for his evocative writings on Wiltshire – but Sussex won him round. And today, despite all the developments and incursions that might threaten the charm of the landscape, the country seems to stay impervious. Parts may be spoiled, but the whole remains very much itself.

Perhaps this is partly because the county, West and East, offers a complete selection box of landscape and views – it can produce something for all tastes, from stony coastlines to rolling downs, and from villages seemingly dug into the land to wide, open vistas. Considered remote and somewhat primitive as recently as the early twentieth century, in more recent years Sussex's proximity to London, its variety of popular seaside towns, and its vastly increased accessibility have failed to compromise its charm. Perhaps this is as much to do with what Sussex doesn't have – no heavy industry, and only two, relatively small, cities – Brighton & Hove, and Chichester. Whatever the reason, the traveller visiting for the first time is bound to be surprised to find how unspoiled large tracts of the landscape still are, and how satisfying an exploration of the varied countryside can be. The Sussex landscape it seems – just like the people – 'wun't be druv'.

SUSSEX STATISTICS

'I love England, especially the English countryside. We had a cottage in Sussex. I love those cottages.'

RICHARD WIDMARK, AMERICAN ACTOR

How long has SUSSEX *been* Sussex? There was a kingdom of the South Saxons from the fifth century onwards, and a document recorded '*Sud Seaxe*' – the South Saxons – in 722. By the time THE DOMESDAY BOOK was being written up in 1086, this had become *Sudsexe*, only a step away from the modern county name.

Two coats of arms

The two parts of the county have had individual coats of arms for centuries. As early as 1611, the RED SHIELD for East Sussex, and the BLUE SHIELD for West Sussex (both with six golden martlets), were in use.

The martlet is a heraldic bird that is always shown without feet, and is often equated with the swallow. In the Sussex arms, the six martlets represent the six ancient 'rapes' or sub-divisions of the country, which existed before the Norman invasion.

Today, each Sussex crest has a golden Saxon crown in its top half, and a wavy line, symbolic of the county's bond with the sea, divides this from the martlets below.

✣ EAST SUSSEX's crest is similar to the banner of the ancient Kingdom of Sussex in the sixth century. It shows a crown above a wavy bar, with six martlets in the lower half. The colours are gold on red.

✣ WEST SUSSEX's version is gold on blue, and also has the martlets and the Saxon crown, but is topped with a crest of oak leaves and acorns. These additions were imported from the Surrey coat of arms when parts of that county were incorporated into West Sussex in 1974. Subsequent redrawings of the county boundaries left Gatwick Airport as the only remaining Surrey takeover within Sussex boundaries, but the oak leaves remain.

One rather complicated pedigree for the martlets claims that they reflect the power of the lords of Arundel in Sussex, the French word for swallow being '*hirondelle*' which sounds like 'Arundel'.

A county divided

Although West and East Sussex were recognised as distinct areas as early as the twelfth century, and were organised as separate entities by the sixteenth, formal separation did not come until the 1880s. In 1888, as a part of the Local Government Act, the two parts were formally divided into two administrations.

Measuring up

✣ **West Sussex** is divided into seven districts:
1. Adur, *2.* Arun, *3.* Chichester, *4.* Crawley, *5.* Horsham, *6.* Mid-Sussex, and *7.* Worthing. Its county town is *Chichester*.

✣ **East Sussex** is divided into six districts:
1. Brighton and Hove, *2.* Eastbourne, *3.* Hastings, *4.* Lewes, *5.* Rother, and *6.* Wealden. Its county town is *Lewes*.

✣ **West Sussex** comes out ahead (it's bigger, has a higher population, and an extra district), but by only a narrow margin.

Place names

Anglo-Saxon place names still rule in Sussex. Here are a few of the commonest prefixes and affixes in original form, with examples of the places by which they are identified:

Becc a brook or stream (*Bexhill*)
Burh a hill, or citadel (*Burghersh, Pulborough*)
Denu a valley (*East Dean, Marden*)
Ea a marsh (*Winchelsea, Selsea*)
Feld a plain or flat place (*Heathfield*)
Folde a field (*Slinfold*)
Ham a village, an enclosure (*Beddingham*)
Hou a hill (*Piddinghoe*)
Hurst a wood (*Nuthurst*)
Ig an island (*Thorney*)
Mersc a marsh (*Peasmarsh*)
Stede a station, a place (*East Grinstead*)
Tun a dwelling, a close (*Alfriston*)
Wic a village, a dwelling place (*Terwick*)

A complete review of English place names was conducted in *The Place Names of Sussex*, published in 1929/30 for the English Place-name Society. Helena Hall published a short version in her update of the Reverend Parish's *Dictionary of Sussex Dialect*, updated in 1957, from which this is a selection.

	Area in sq km	*Ranked in England & Wales*	*Population in 2005*	*Ranked in England & Wales*
✣ **West Sussex**	*1,991*	30th in size	*764,300*	27th in size
✣ **East Sussex**	*1,792*	33rd in size	*752,900*	28th in size

MORE STATISTICS

The South Downs Way

THE SOUTH DOWNS WAY, stretching between Water Lane in Winchester in Hampshire and the west end of the seaside promenade in Eastbourne in East Sussex, is one of the best-known walkers' paths in Britain. Measuring around 100 miles (160km) from one end to the other, it covers the landscapes of both East and West Sussex in all its variety, and covers a large chunk of Hampshire for good measure. Its highest point is DITCHLING BEACON, at 814ft (248m), and it passes near to most of the county's most scenic spots and interesting towns.

UNUSUAL HERITAGE

Something that has shaped the history of Sussex and many of her great estates is the unusual inheritance practice of BOROUGH ENGLISH. *Technically known as ultimogeniture, this means that the youngest surviving son of a family inherits its estate – the opposite of the far more common state of primogeniture. This has been a marked custom from medieval times. It is not unique to Sussex (parts of Middlesex, Suffolk and Surrey also use it), but it is unusual in Britain overall.*

Sussex wildlife

Sussex is rich in FAUNA and FLORA, and some plants and insects that are quite easily found there are rare or (in formal terms) 'nationally scarce' elsewhere. The top ten in this category in the Sussex Rare Species Inventory are:

- ROUND-HEADED RAMPION (*Phyteuma orbiculare*, see p18)
- FROGBIT (*Hydrocharis morus-ranae*, waterplant, also known as waterpoppy)
- ADONIS BLUE (*Lysandra bellargus*, butterfly)
- LONG-WINGED CONEHEAD (*Conocephalus discolor*, cricket)
- DOOR SNAIL (*Macrogastra rolphii*)
- HAIRY DRAGONFLY (*Brachytron pratense*)
- RUDDY DARTER (*Sympetrum sanguineum*, dragonfly)
- VARIABLE DAMSELFLY (*Coenagrion pulchellum*)
- WHITE-LEGGED DAMSELFLY (*Platycnemis pennipes*)
- DOWNY EMERALD (*Cordulea aenea*, dragonfly)

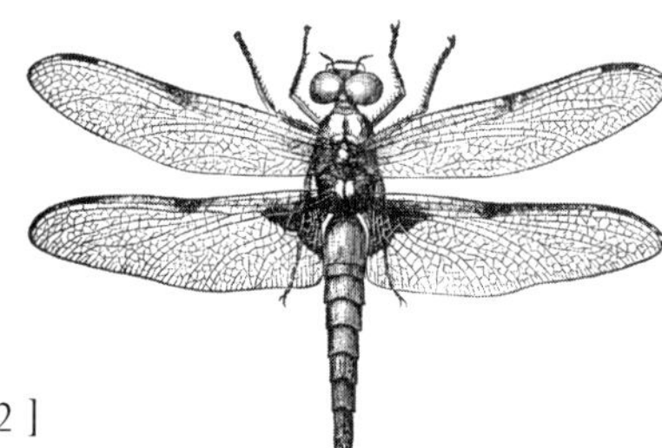

Saxon Sussex

Even career historians have problems sorting out the early rule of Sussex. We know that the SAXONS were making inroads into southern England by the third century because the Romans were building forts to protect the coast against them, but these early Germanic invaders didn't arrive, like DUKE WILLIAM OF NORMANDY, in one neat fleet with a date. Instead they gradually took over, and although the history between the third and the ninth century has numerous gaps, it tells of increasing Saxon influence.

The source of much early information is the ANGLO-SAXON CHRONICLE, a text that was compiled entry by entry between the earliest years after Christ and the twelfth century, but which can largely be dated back to a manuscript dated 891. It was much added-to over the centuries and little of the text it contains can be independently verified, but it claims that a figure called Ælle became first bretwalda – chief or king – of the South Saxons in the fifth century.

A list of some of the indefinite rulers from this vague period of history follows, partly because of the wonderful resonance of the Anglo-Saxon names, and partly because it demonstrates that power was in a constant state of flux.

☛ *Many of the reigns overlap, sometimes because power was shared, sometimes because the records mention more than one leader for the period in question:*

DATE OF REIGN	*King, bretwalda or ealdorman*
?c.660-?c.685	*Ædelwealh*
?c.683	*Eadwulf*
?c.683-?c.685	*Ecgwald*
?c.685	*Andhun*

✣ From *c.*686 to 726, the kingdom came under the overall rule of neighbouring Wessex:

692-717	*Nodhelm*
692-700	*Watt*
717	*Aedelstan*
740	*Aedelberht*
760-772	*Osmund*

✣ From 771 to 825, the kingdom was placed under the rule of Mercia:

772	*Oswald*
765-772	*Oslac*
765-791	*Ealdwulf*
765-772	*Ælfwald*

✣ From 825, the kingdom was back under Wessex:

825-839	*Ecgberht*
839-858	*Ethulwulf*
858-865	*Ethulbert*
865-871	*Ethelred*

✣ On the death of ETHELRED, we finally get back into more familiar territory with the accession of his son, who became ALFRED THE GREAT.

SUSSEX FOSSILS

'His rise and fall are a salutary example of human motive, mischief and mistake...'

EDITORIAL ON PILTDOWN MAN, *NATURE*, 1954

Sussex is particularly rich in FOSSILS, but for centuries the local people who came across them, lying among rockfall on the shore, or under the blades of their ploughs, did not know how to identify them, believing them to be giants' bones, or dragons' teeth (which, of course, in a sense, they were). Fittingly, it was a Sussex man, the doctor and naturalist GIDEON MANTELL, who was one of the first to attempt to categorise his findings into a specific sort of animal.

SITE	*PERIOD OF FOSSILS*	*HOW LONG AGO?*
Bracklesham Bay	*Eocene*	40-50 million
Eastbourne	*Cretaceous*	85 million
Folkestone	*Cretaceous*	100 million
Hastings	*Early cretaceous*	140 million
Littlehampton	*Cretaceous*	75-100 million
Peacehaven	*Late Cretaceous*	80-85 million
Seaford	*Cretaceous*	70-100 million
Seven Sisters	*Cretaceous*	70-100 million

Eight great fossil sites

Should you want to fossil-hunt, check the rules first: some sites encourage amateurs, others forbid them!

The immense lengths of the classified prehistoric periods are almost impossible to grasp. The CRETACEOUS period overall lasted just over 71 million years, so the dates given in the table relate to the fossils actually found on each site – to the nearest five million years or so.

Ammonite houses

Falling outside the familiar architectural orders, a sudden – and brief – fashion for capitals in the form of AMMONITES (those curled shell fossils found all along the rocky Sussex coastline) flourished in the early nineteenth century. Just a few appeared in London, but the Sussex father-and-son builders, AMON WILDS & AMON HENRY WILDS, introduced a number in fossil-mad Sussex, including them on terraces in Brighton and, in Lewes, on the elegant façade of Castle Place on Lewes High Street. It may be that they appreciated the pun of Amonnite on their name, or they may simply have been following the contemporary craze for antiquarian themes in their work.

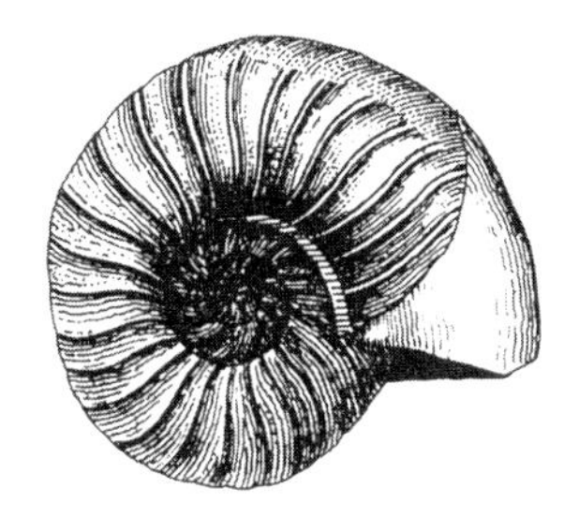

The Piltdown scandal

One of the most famous associations between palaeontology and Sussex is the discovery – and later discrediting – of 'the man who never was': PILTDOWN MAN. No-one knows for sure who perpetrated the fraud, but in 1912, CHARLES DAWSON, a respected bone-hunter uncovered a skull at Piltdown which seemed to combine the characteristics of earlier and later specimens, having the large cranium and high forehead of modern man and a primitive jaw much closer to Neanderthal remains. Dawson died in 1916, and by the early 1950s the skull (and a later example, also uncovered at Piltdown by Dawson) had been discredited, and it was acknowledged that *Eoanthropus dawsoni* had actually been formed from the top part of a human skull and the jawbone of an orang utan. Who perpetrated the fraud, and why, has never been established – suspects have ranged from Dawson himself to a number of his colleagues, and the list even includes an intriguing appearance from SIR ARTHUR CONAN DOYLE, himself an amateur palaeontologist.

The naming of parts

It was GIDEON MANTELL, a Sussex doctor, who 'created' the first named dinosaur. An enthusiastic naturalist and fossil hunter, when huge teeth and bone fossils were found at Cuckfield in the early 1820s, he noticed that they resembled those of the iguana, but were around twenty times the size. From this came the name IGUANADON, used ever since. The term 'dinosaur', from the Greek *deinos*, 'fearfully great' and *sauros*, 'lizard', was coined in 1842 by the scientist RICHARD OWEN.

THE BRICKWORKS DINOSAUR

The village of Rudgwick has its very own dinosaur, the remains of which were found in the local brickworks in 1985. In 1996, Polacanthus rudgwickensis *was acknowledged with its own classification – it was an armour-plated, spike-backed herbivore, resembling a five-ton armadillo. Its remains can be seen in the museum at Horsham.*

THE SUSSEX COASTLINE

'When I gaze on the sea, I want to be on it, over it, across it – there is no home for me here'

CHARLES LAMB

Rocky and rugged, with shingle beaches often overhung by towering cliffs, the Sussex coastline is just as picturesque as the DOWNLAND LANDSCAPE, and can offer as much in terms of folklore and history. The play of light on the coastal landscape inspired TURNER, among others, to create lasting memorials of its splendour. The more pragmatic smugglers and fishermen looked instead at what trade could be brought from the sea.

The Sussex Cinque Ports

Because more than five names crop up whenever the CINQUE PORTS are discussed, there is sometimes confusion as to which are the 'real' ports.

The original five, granted privileges in return for maintaining ships for the king's use if necessary, were: **1.** HASTINGS, **2.** NEW ROMNEY, **3.** HYTHE, **4.** DOVER and **5.** SANDWICH – so only one, Hastings, was in Sussex. As time went on and the trade in the ports grew, names were added to the list – RYE and WINCHELSEA became Cinque Ports, also, and a number of 'Limbs' were added as extensions to existing members.

A government post, Lord Warden of the Cinque Ports, was created at some point in the twelfth century; the office still exists, with an official residence at Walmer Castle, but is now solely an honorary role.

Smuggling in Sussex

SMUGGLING was one of the foremost businesses in Sussex through the eighteenth and much of the nineteenth century. One nineteenth-century wit claimed that all Sussex men were either shepherds or smugglers.

Here are some facts & terms

[**OWLING**] the original term for smuggling, referring first purely to the smuggling of wool.

[**TUBBING**] the conveyance of contraband goods in 'tubs', often disguised with a top layer of licit goods.

[**DERRICKING**] the technique by which goods were hauled up a cliff face from an inaccessible beach.

[**CONDEMNED HOLE**] the dump in Hastings where the remains of smugglers' boats were left, having been cut into pieces. In fact, the upended bows and sterns of the boats were often used to make huts for the town's fishermen

[150] the total number of excisemen employed by the government to foil smuggling in Sussex and Kent in the early eighteenth century. At this period, the number of smugglers pitted against them was probably in the thousands.

[3 MILLION] the number of pounds of tea it is estimated were smuggled in the first half of the eighteenth century. This was three times the total of tea brought in legally.

The strange lure of Beachy Head

BEACHY HEAD is one of the most beautiful places on one of the prettiest stretches of coastline in southern England. Why it should also have become one of Britain's most popular locations for would-be suicides remains a mystery, but records stretching back to the seventeenth century show that people have always seen it as a jumping site as well as a beauty spot. In more recent times the mere fact that it is known to be popular with would-be suicides probably only increases its charm. And the numbers seemed bent on rising: from an average of 6-7 deaths per year in the 1950s, the figure had risen to an average of 17 by the end of the 1990s. However the trend may recently have been reversed – after further rises between 2002 and 2005, a steep decrease to only 7 deaths in 2006 has been attributed to the CHAPLAINCY TEAM, a band of volunteers linked to a number of local churches, who patrol the clifftop during the day and into the evening. There is also a strategically sited telephone box with a hotline direct to the SAMARITANS, the charity that helps those in emotional distress. With ever-increased efforts in place, over time Beachy Head may regain its role as a breathtaking beauty spot – and no more than that.

How to make Brighton rock

How do the letters get into the rock? It's complicated:

1. *Boil water, sugar and glucose syrup until it coagulates into candy.*

2. *Colour quantities of the mixture with red and pink, leaving the largest quantity white. Work while the candy is still warm.*

3. *Make each letter by putting together small units of square-ended red candy rods two metres long into the shape of the letter. Support the shape with rods of plain white candy.*

4. *When all the letters have been formed, put them around a circular rod of plain white candy. Separate them with more rods of plain white.*

5. *Roll the 'pipe' of rock in a border of plain white candy.*

6. *Roll the 'pipe' of rock in an outer, very thin layer of pink candy.*

7. *Pull the rock out until it is the right diameter.*

8. *Chop the cylinder into the foot-long sticks of classic seaside rock.*

SUSSEX FLORA

'If you look at the flowers with the sun before you, they appear like shining gems sewn into the fabric [of the Downs]'

W.H. HUDSON, *NATURE IN DOWNLAND*, 1923

The mild climate of the county and the regular rainfall ensures that the range of WILD PLANTS and FLOWERS is broad and healthy. Sussex has high numbers of plants that are rare elsewhere (of the 50 orchid species growing wild in Britain the county is home to 33), and, despite its proximity to London and the inroads made on its unspoiled land, it still also offers plenty of undisturbed sites kept as nature reserves for both plants and animals.

The Himalayas in Sussex

Kew Gardens' outpost at WAKEHURST PLACE reported that the heatwave of 2006 had provoked only the second known flowering of the rare *Clematis zemuensis*, a delicate white-flowered climbing plant with an elusive scent, found naturally only in the Himalayas. No other examples of this plant, much less one in flower, have been reported anywhere else in the British Isles.

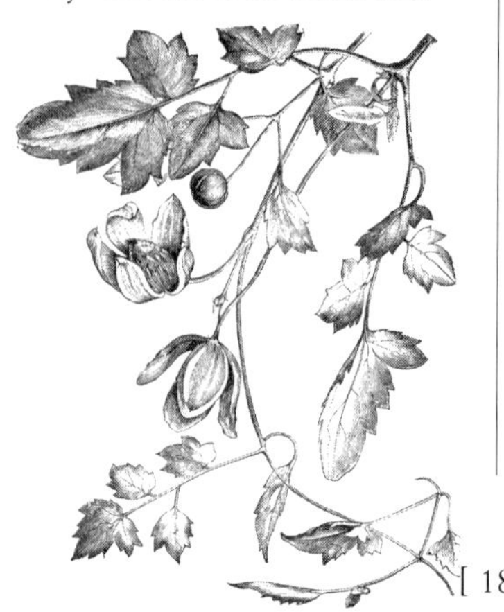

Masters of disguise

Sussex is home to the BEE-ORCHID (*Ophrys apifera*), one of the oddest members of an eccentric family. Not only do the orchid's flowers cunningly disguise themselves as bees, but they also secrete a smell that resembles natural bee pheromones strongly enough to confuse the – usually discriminating – insects. Failed attempts to mate with the flowers lead to the male bees departing disappointed, but coated with pollen – all the better to fertilise the next bee-orchid to attract them.

The devil's plaything

YARROW, also known as 'the devil's plaything' and a key ingredient in many spells and charms, and revered in the past as a holy plant, has an odd reputation, believed to be excellent medicine, but unlucky in certain applications. It stops bleeding and lowers fevers, and a bunch tied to a baby's cradle will repel witches and bad luck, yet it is still sometimes regarded with unease. Unique to Sussex is the belief that it should not be planted on a young man's grave for fear of giving him unquiet dreams and not allowing the dead to rest.

THE COUNTY FLOWER

*The round-headed rampion (*Phyteuma orbiculare*), known as the Pride of Sussex, is the county's flower. It's an attractive but unkempt-looking plant with pretty, shaggy blue flowers. It grows to about 1ft 6in (45cm) tall, with oval leaves and long, thready stems. Once common across the south of England, it is increasingly rare, though still quite often found in Sussex itself.*

Terms for common plants

A list taken from the REVEREND W. PARISH's well-known dictionary of Sussex local dialect:

- ALE HOOF or LION'S MOUTH
  Ground ivy
- APPLE-PIE
  Hairy willow herb
- BETHWINE OR TOMBACCA
  Wild clematis, Old Man's Beard
- BREAD-AND-CHEESE
  Hawthorn buds
- BUTTER-AND-EGGS OR PIG'S PETTITOE
  Bird's foot trefoil
- COLE
  Sea kale
- DEAD MEN'S FINGERS
  Purple orchid
- GOLD CUP
  Buttercup
- GRANDMOTHER'S PINCUSHION
  Field scabious
- KISS-ME
  Wild viola
- RABBIT'S-MEAT
  Wild parsley

and, to finish, one insect – in old Sussex, the ladybird is known as:

- 'GOD ALMIGHTY'S COW'

SUSSEX FAUNA

'Sing Ho! For the life of a Bear!'

A.A. MILNE, *WINNIE THE POOH*, 1926

With its varied and fertile terrain, Sussex has played host to many incoming species as well as to its own native populations of animals and birds. If they pick their spot carefully, visitors may have sight of WALLABIES and WILD BOAR as well as those of the rabbits and field mice they might more reasonably expect.

The 'Hastings rarities'

Raising a scandal that rumbled on in the ornithology world from the 1930s to the 1960s, the story of the Hastings Rarities revolved around the unassuming taxidermy shop of GEORGE BRISTOW, at 15 Silchester Road, St Leonards. Between the 1890s and the 1930s, Bristow sold a wide range of birds, allegedly all locally acquired (both as skins and stuffed specimens) to collectors and ornithologists. From the 1930s onwards, the unusually high incidence of birds previously unknown in Sussex but sold by Bristow as local provoked rumours of fraud. The taxidermist indignantly refuted any accusations (and himself asked, if the birds in question did not come from Sussex, where did anyone imagine he had got them?). Nonetheless, the amount his sales of rarities raised was considerable for the time, and after his death in 1947 the questions rumbled on. Finally two articles in the well-regarded periodical *British Birds* in 1962 flatly recommended that a number of the birds sold by Bristow – 16 species and 13 sub-species – be removed from the official records, as it was simply too statistically unlikely that they had genuinely been obtained in Sussex. This created a lasting confusion, because many publications on British birds had incorporated species which could only have been verified by Bristow. The puzzle was never satisfactorily explained, and the case never resolved either for or against. Of the full species dropped from the record, 13 have subsequently been reinstated after reliable sightings were reported. A number of Bristow's birds can still be seen in the museum at Hastings.

The sixteen dubious rarities

- *Black Lark* – since relisted
- *Brown Flycatcher*
- *Calendra Lark* – since relisted
- *Cetti's Warbler* – since relisted
- *Collared Flycatcher* – since relisted
- *Cory's Shearwater* – since relisted
- *Grey-tailed Tattler* – since relisted
- *Masked Shrike* – since relisted
- *Moustached Warbler*
- *Olivaceous Warbler* – since relisted
- *Rueppell's Warbler* – since relisted
- *Sardinian Warbler* – since relisted
- *Semipalmated Sandpiper* – since relisted
- *Slender-billed Curlew* – since relisted
- *Terek Sandpiper* – since relisted
- *White-winged Snowfinch*

A famous bear & wallabies

ASHDOWN FOREST has long been known to fans of A. A. MILNE as the playground of CHRISTOPHER ROBIN and WINNIE THE POOH. But between the 1940s and the 1970s, it was also home to a colony of wallabies, probably escaped pets, which naturalised in the area (they may have provided Milne with the inspiration for Kanga and Roo). From first sightings in 1942, they appeared to die off, and no confirmed sightings have now been reported for over 30 years. If you want to see wallabies in natural surroundings in Sussex, however, there is a healthy colony living in LEONARDSLEE GARDENS at Lower Beeding, near Horsham.

Alien big cats

'ABCs' as they are known to connoisseurs of the mysterious, are sighted in Sussex at a particularly high rate. Here is a partial – only a partial – record of sightings for 1999, originally published in the *Fortean Times*:

8 January – Sightings in Ringmer, Rodmell and East Chiltington
February – Sighting in Wilson Avenue, Lewes
8 March – Adversane, off the B2133 'Beige ABC with tufts on ears and tail'
13 March – Sighting at East Chiltington
April – Sighting at Chailey 'Fitting the description of a jaguarundi'
2 April – Firle, 1.5-in talon found in field
7 May – Cuckfield, ABC seen at distance of five yards
Mid-May – Two sightings at Burgess Hill
23 May – Sighting at Holton St Mary, near Hassocks
Early July – Sighting at Newchapel. Two sheep attacked in a manner typical of a big cat
September – Sighting half a mile from the Ashcombe roundabout near Lewes
Early October – Cuckfield Lane, Warninglid, sighting of a small 'lioness'
6 December – Sighting near Bramber, 'lioness' seen at 30-40 ft.

RIVERS, LAKES & PONDS

'Only the dewpond on the height
Unfed that never fails....'

RUDYARD KIPLING, *SUSSEX, 1901*

If the landscape of Sussex strikes one as being mainly of chalk (as well it might), then WATER, too, plays a big part in the county's life and looks. Five large RIVERS meander down to the coast, and Sussex also has a long coastline. Areas of enclosed water, too, are everywhere, from the surprising DEWPOND that one comes across on a high point of the Downs to the LAKES and MOATS around the large estates in the county.

The five principal rivers of Sussex

RIVER	*SOURCE*	*MOUTH*
Adur	*south of Horsham*	Shoreham
Arun	*St Leonard's Forest*	Littlehampton
Cuckmere	*north of Heathfield*	Cuckmere Haven
Ouse	*near Beeding*	Newhaven
Rother	*Rotherfield*	Rye

☛ *The Cuckmere is the only one of the five that does not have a port at its mouth.*
☛ *The Rother should not be confused with the river of the same name in West Sussex. The West Sussex Rother runs across Hampshire into Sussex, eventually joining the River Arun.*

The dewponds of the Downs

DEWPONDS are used to water animals high on the hills where there are no convenient streams or rivers to drink from. No-one knows how old the technique of making a dewpond is, but Sussex still has a fair few, though many have vanished through neglect since sheep farming became less of a focus in the county.

At one time the land west of the Ouse was called the '*mutton barracks*' on account of the sheer numbers of sheep that were grazed there.

Whatever legend may say, dew ponds don't occur naturally, nor are they really exclusively dew fed. Traditionally they are made in dry weather:

1. *Dig out a broad, dish-shaped, shallow indentation in the chalk. It should be no more than 3ft deep at its deepest point, and can be as shallow as 2ft.*
2. *Line the pond with a layer of straw. Stamp it down, or get your cattle to do the job for you.*
3. *Cover the straw with clay, in a thick layer. Stamp it down well to make a solid lining without cracks or gaps. 'Puddle' it (stamp it down) hard, or put your cattle to work again.*
4. *Leave to dry. After three weeks the pond will fill, and after that it will not dry out.*

While condensed dew was probably responsible for some of the water in the pond, most came from rainfall. Ponds usually only dried out when weeds and reeds were not removed regularly; eventually their roots cracked the clay lining and the water drained away.

GILBERT WHITE, the celebrated naturalist, notes that one typical dew pond (although not in Sussex) was 'never above three feet deep in the middle, and not more than 30 feet in diameter, and contained perhaps not more than two or three hogsheads of water, yet it is never known to fail, though it affords drink to 300 or 400 sheep and for at least 20 herds of cattle besides.'

Sussex watermills

Every Sussex river had its WATERMILLS in the past, and some had many – for example even the Western Rother, a relatively small river, once had thirteen spaced along it, of which the last, TERWICK MILL, closed in 1966. **NB:** *Six Sussex watermills can still be visited, though, and seen in action.*

1. **Park Mill**, *Bateman's, Burwash*
   Dating from the 1750s, this mill is adjacent to Kipling's last Sussex home and features in a number of his stories.
2. **Burton Watermill**, *south of Petworth* Dates from 1784.
3. **Coultershaw Beam Pump**, *near Petworth*
   An unusual 'mill', built in 1782 to pump up a supply of water for Petworth house and town.
4. **Ifield Watermill**
   Dating from 1684, but rebuilt and modernised in 1817.
5. **Lurgashall Watermill**, *Weald & Downland Open Air Museum, Singleton*
   Dating from the seventeenth century, and given to the museum in 1973. Flour ground at the mill is sold in the museum shop.
6. **Michelham Priory Watermill**
   Restructured in 1896 and fully working today.

CHAPTER TWO

MYTHICAL SUSSEX

Saints and sinners, dragons and devils, giants, witches, warlocks and monsters all loom large in Sussex lore, and you'll find a broad selection in the following pages. The characteristic county response is largely robust, and often irreverent – the devil is sent off with a flea in his ear, both witch and monster are defeated by cunning yokels with a brain in their heads, and the memorable thing about the most intensely Sussex saint is that he wheeled his aged mother around in a barrow. Hearteningly level-headed, all of them – even the seventeenth-century gutter press description of the 'serpente' to be encountered in St Leonard's Forest doesn't descend into risible exaggeration, instead noting cautiously that it hasn't yet grown wings, but is showing symptoms of developing them. A robust approach and a good sense of humour seem to be the weapons most relied upon to defeat these creatures that are bound to appear now and then.

A different, much more tragic kind of mythology surrounds the period when religious dissension in the country at large broke into Sussex's self-contained shell. The Sussex martyrs, in the main family people with a calm but obstinate adherence to their right to worship in their own tongue, are still remembered here when others elsewhere in the country are often forgotten. Their biggest memorial is the annual madness that is Bonfire Night in Lewes, and there is a sort of justice in the fact that it's this wild event that is most likely to set up its own mythology in the twenty-first century.

SUSSEX GHOSTS & DRAGONS

'A serpent in every stream...'

ANONYMOUS

Sussex is not short of MONSTERS – and many of them are not in human form. Some of them are not alive, either. DRAGONS, SERPENTS, and many less identifiable BEASTS lurk in every coppice and haunt every dewpond. If you are moving off the beaten track, step carefully – legend tells us that you may encounter all manner of wildlife, including species that don't appear in most reputable field guides. Consider this section as an awful warning; tread softly, and carry a big stick...

The defeat of the Knucker

Well-known in local lore, the KNUCKER is a monster both fearsome and funny; living in a bottomless pond, known as a knuckerhole, near Lyminster, this water dragon regularly devoured local people and livestock, but, in the most popular version of the story, was defeated by a local man (*Jim Pulk*, *Polk*, or *Puttock* – the name varies in the different tellings), who cooked him an immense and indigestible pie liberally laced with poison, and hauled it to the hole with the help of a horse and cart. The Knucker swallowed pie, horse and conveyance and died in agony. Unfortunately so did the cunning killer, who had somehow accidentally ingested some of the poison himself. A medieval grave marker, known as the SLAYER'S SLAB, can be seen in Lyminster Church – although it is not known whose grave it really marks.

The St Leonard's monster

The sensational stories of the red-top press are nothing new – in 1614 a pamphlet was published that gave a very full account of the DRAGON of St Leonard's Forest, appropriately enough near the village of Dragon's Green. The writer did not hold back:

'This serpente... is reputed to nine feete... in length... a quantitie of thickness in the middest and somewhat smaller at both endes. The former parte, which he shootes forth as a necke, is supposed to be an elle long... The scales along his back seem to be blackish, and so much as is discovered under his bellie appeareth to be red... He rids always as fast as a man can run. There are likewise upon either side of him discovered two great bunches so big as a large foote-ball, and (as some thinke) will in time grow to wings'.

The writer ended with the pious desire that,

> *'God, I hope, will… that he be destroyed before he grows to fledge'.*

No more was heard of the monster, so perhaps he got his wish.

Black dogs & grey ladies

Sussex has no shortage of either ghostly GREY LADIES or spectral BLACK DOGS. Many of the former are found in castles and ancient ruins; the latter mostly appear on lonely downland and deserted paths.

Six grey ladies

1. *Hastings Castle has a grey lady carrying a baby. She is believed to be a suicidal servant girl, who killed both herself and her illegitimate baby.*

2. *Tuckvar House in Alfriston boasts a tall ghostly woman who is seen wandering up and down the stairs and in the larder.*

3. *The inn at Blackboys is haunted by a quiet phantom, believed to be that of a lady who died in childbed.*

4. *Michelham Priory has a grey lady in Tudor dress.*

5. *The lady in grey at Beachy Head is, unsurprisingly, thought to be the ghost of another suicide. There are stories of her bending to greet the pet dogs of the living – who run away, howling with fear.*

6. *The grey lady of Pevensey Castle is seen walking the parapets in fading light. She is believed to be the ghost of Lady Pelham, a supporter of the Earl of Bolingbroke in the conflict for England's crown at the end of the fourteenth century.*

Four black dogs

M.A. LOWER, a celebrated antiquarian of Sussex, writing in the mid-nineteenth century, wrote that

> *'every unfrequented corner has its Demon in the form of a Black Dog'*

– a remark worthy of that scholar of the sinister, M.R. JAMES. These manifestations are certainly common in the countryside. Four of the best:

1. *A headless version runs around Black Dog Hill, on the Westmeston-Ditchling road.*

2. *Alfriston has two phantom dogs, one black, one white. The black dog runs down into the village from the Downs; the white one, an altogether tamer prospect, was the pet of a young local man, murdered alongside his master, and remaining vigilant at the scene of the crime.*

3. *A black dog walks the hills above the Long Man, carved into the Downs at Wilmington. This is a good spot for the supernatural, being the site of several ancient barrows.*

4. *Henfield Woods have one of the most frightening manifestations – an immense black hound with blood-red eyes.*

SUSSEX GIANTS & MONSTERS

'The Giant keeps his secret and from his hillside flings out a perpetual challenge.'

THE REV. A. EVANS, THE LONG MAN OF WILMNGTON

GIANTS surely once walked the Sussex Downs – so many traces and legends persist. Most have left a benign heritage, casually amending the landscape, or leaving a handful of immense artifacts to remind us of their time here. The hills are scattered with the barrows that legend tells us are giants' graves. Just a few are remembered in a less friendly way, with fearful habits and a shadowy legacy of myth and legend.

Bevis of Hampton

BEVIS is far from an exclusively Sussex giant (the Hampton in his name refers to present-day Southampton, and the original chivalric romance that bears his name has been translated into languages including Italian and Yiddish), but he has nonetheless left his mark on the county. The original of the legend probably lived during the tenth century, but the oldest recorded manuscript version of his story dates to the 1400s, and has him as the son of GUY OF HAMPTON. His mother is a princess of Scotland, but organises the death of his father and marries his killer, exiling Bevis to the court of the KING OF ARMENIA. After many adventures, including battles with a dragon and a man-eating wild boar, and marriage to the king's daughter, JOSIAN, Bevis eventually dies at more or less the same time as his wife and his noble horse, HIRONDELLE. Despite the range of his travels, Bevis has two graves in England, one the long barrow in the park of ARUNDEL CASTLE. His sword, MORGLAY, is kept in the armoury of the castle, and measures 5ft 9in – which would seem to confirm his giant status. His horse, Hirondelle in the French legend, seems to be named after the town of Arundel (or was the town named for the horse?). Finally, another barrow, at nearby Compton village, is known as BEVIS'S THUMB.

VARIATIONS ON BEVIS'S NAME

Anglo-Norman	*Boeve de Haumlone*
Early English	*Sir Boues of Hamtoun*
French	*Beuve d'Hanstone*
Italian	*Buovo d'Antona*
Yiddish	*Bovo-Bukh*

The ogre of Brede

Despite a fearsome reputation, SIR GODDARD OXENBRIDGE, the ogre of Brede, who died in 1487, is buried quietly in the village church alongside his wife. How the awful stories that grew up about him is unclear – gigantic in stature, he was alleged in his lifetime to be a witch, and to kidnap and dine on children. He could not be killed in any ordinary way, but the children of the neighbourhood eventually brewed a vast vat of beer, waited until he was drunk, then cut him in half with a wooden saw. His bloodstains are said still to be visible at the GROANING BRIDGE in Stubb's Lane, Brede, scene of the crime.

Of an immense size

The largest GIANT in Sussex – in England, too – is purely two dimensional. Measuring 235ft from the soles of his feet to the top of his head, the LONG MAN OF WILMINGTON appears to be striding across the Downs above the village that gives him his name. Not much is known of his origins – the earliest recording of him is a drawing made in 1710, and seems to show him as a more shadowy figure. Theories vary from prehistoric fertility figure to Roman war god, or seventeenth-century fantasy – whatever the truth, the current outline, reinforced by a line of cream-painted blocks, was marked in 1874 with yellow bricks (replaced in the 1970s). He has looked out over Sussex ever since, apart from a brief period during World War II, when he was painted green to avoid enemy planes using him as a landmark.

A real monster

In the late 1940s, a genuine monster came to Sussex. His name was JOHN GEORGE HAIGH, but today he's better remembered by his enduring soubriquet – *The Acid Bath Murderer*. Despite a plea of insanity, he seems to have murdered purely for money, dissolving his six known victims in a 'bath' of sulphuric acid. Two died at a tiny workshop he rented in Crawley, he was charged at Horsham, and his trial took place at Lewes Crown Court. His description of the overwhelming urge that came over him to drink his victims' blood failed to convince the jury and he was found guilty and hanged on 10 August 1949, reported as cheerful and impervious to the end.

☛ *Among his last acts was to pose for a death mask for Madame Tussaud's, to whom he had already bequeathed a suit of clothes for his waxwork, which was to appear in their Chamber of Horrors.*

WITCHES & WARLOCKS

'I saw...something that was real and very potent.
I saw the world of force behind the world of form.'

DOREEN VALIENTE, SUSSEX WITCH

Within the folklore of Sussex there are plenty of records of WITCHES and WARLOCKS, and the county has a more recent history of WITCHCRAFT which its followers take very seriously. The county featured prominently in the witchcraft assizes of the seventeenth century, with bizarre accounts of familiars, ranging in form from hares to weasels and imps, wreaking havoc on the innocent. These days you're unlikely to encounter witchcraft unless you go looking for it, but there are enough ley lines and ancient sites to attract plenty of mystical practice to Sussex.

The wickedest man in the world

ALEISTER CROWLEY would probably have dubbed himself a mystic and a magician rather than a witch, but the string of scandals in which he played a starring role and many of which he engineered were long over by the time he came to Sussex. In 1945 he moved into Netherwood, a boarding house on The Ridge in Hastings, run by Mrs Kathleen Symonds and her husband Vernon, making a final gesture towards the excesses of earlier years by choosing room number 13. Expelled from Italy by Mussolini, revelling in his title of 'THE GREAT BEAST', Crowley, regarded by many as a key figure in the revival and recasting of modern 'magick' was reduced to joining the Hastings Chess Club and managing his drug addiction with regular deliveries of heroin from a London chemist. In spare moments he tutored the Symonds' nephew in Latin and chatted to the handsome white rabbits kept by Vernon in the back garden. He died, generally regretted by the household, on 1 December 1947. Mrs Symonds remembered the Great Beast as an excellent tenant and great fun.

Hitler versus the Sussex witches

One of the most bizarre stories centred around ASHDOWN FOREST, is that in 1940 a coven met there led by GERALD GARDNER, the man subsequently known as the father of modern witchcraft, and summoned a Cone of Power to defeat HITLER. This was a ceremony so secret that the details are scant, but that had historically been credited by witches for the defeat of the Spanish Armada, and subsequently that of NAPOLEON – now that England was threatened again, the Cone, which somehow harnessed the force of the gathered witches, was summoned once more to repel the threatened invader. The story was never substantiated by Gardner, but, after all, Hitler never did invade, though whether this had anything to do with Sussex witchcraft remains unproven.

The witch of Ditchling

THE DITCHLING WITCH makes regular appearances in Sussex folklore. She's not credited with any very high level of ill-doing, but she had the power to stop any cart dead in front of her cottage on Ditchling Common – and it would not start again until she released it. As in so many folk stories her power was broken by a cunning everyman figure, 'the carter wot knew', who cut the spokes of the wheels of his cart as it stood frozen in front of the witch's house. The witch rushed out of her door, waving her hands, and for every spoke the carter had cut, there was a deep, bloody cut on one of her fingers. After this the witch seems to have given up causing mischief – but how the carter just 'knew' is never revealed.

The Witches' rune

Darksome night and shining moon,
East, then north, then west, then south,
Hearken to the witches' rune
Here I come to call these forth.
Earth and Water, Air and Fire,
Wand and pentacle and sword,
Work ye unto my desire,
Hearken ye unto my work,
Cords and censer, scourge and knife,
Powers of the witches' blade,
Waken all ye unto life,
Come ye as the charm is made.
Queen of Heaven, Queen of Hell,
Horned hunter of the night,
Lend your power unto my spell,
And work my will by magick rite.
By all the power of land and sea,
By all the might of moon and sun,
As I do so mote it be,
Chant the spell and be it done.
Eko, Eko Azarak, Eko, Eko Zamilak, Eko,
Eko Osiris, Eko, Eko Isis

This chant is believed to have been written in the 1950s by DOREEN VALIENTE, a writer, poet and well-respected witch who lived in Brighton and died in 1999. Valiente was known for making the aims of witchcraft sensible to a modern, not necessarily sympathetic audience.

SUSSEX SUPERSTITIONS

'Only women folk sow parsley seed'

TRADITIONAL SUSSEX LORE

Sussex SUPERSTITIONS cover every aspect of life from the first cuckoo's call to the productivity in the bee hive. Alongside all the beliefs linked to the cycle and everyday events of rural life are numerous more unholy beliefs. THE DEVIL features as regularly in superstition as he does in myth, but fortunately the native Sussex wit is usually ahead of him.

Telling the bees

A CUSTOM prevalent in, but not limited to, Sussex was the 'TELLING OF THE BEES' of any important event. If the bees weren't formally told, they would withhold their honey from the skeps' owners. More extreme – and more specific to Sussex – is the belief that if there was a death in the family, a black crêpe bow must be put on each hive, or the bees will die in sympathy. This custom was recorded as still in practice as late as 1948.

The presence of fairies

Sussex has a name among folklorists for being thick with FAIRIES. The high incidence of one of the Anglo-Saxon words for fairy or other-worldly being is '*puca*', developed into *Puck*, *Pook* or *Poch* (the source of KIPLING's *Puck of Pook's Hill*), is said to prove the point. Just a handful of examples found by MAWER & STENTION:

- *Pookhill* or *Poukehale* between Selmeston and Alciston
- *Puckstye* Farm in Hartfield
- *Puxsty* Wood near Wadhurst
- *Pokerlee* Farm in Henfield
- *Puckscroft* in Rusper
- *Pucksroad*, a stream in Cuckfield, crossed by *Pookeborne* Bridge.

The earliest use of the word in a Sussex place name is in the eighth century; a charter describing the boundary of an estate west of Bexhill marks a point as '*Pucan Wylle*', which can be translated as fairy spring.

Chanctonbury Ring

No site in Sussex is surrounded with more legend, superstition and myth than CHANCTONBURY RING, sited between Washington and Wiston in East Sussex. To the casual gaze it's simply a picturesque hill fort with a ring of trees (less dense than before the great storm of 1987) at its summit; to its devotees it is a mystical site where almost anything supernatural can happen. The first ring of beech trees, which give the Ring much of its mysterious atmosphere, was planted in 1760 by CHARLES GORING, the son of the Goring family who lived at WISTON HOUSE nearby. It was not an easy job; water had to be carried manually up the hill to water the seedlings, but the result was a dense plantation crowning the fort, and the birth of numerous myths about the entities to be found there, few of them human. Although many of the trees were blown down in the 1987 hurricane, they have since been replanted by a descendant of the original Charles Goring. And the decimation of the trees did nothing to remove the uncanniness surrounding the site. Everything from UFOs to levitation has been reported from within the ring, and the parties of researchers into the supernatural who regularly visit it rarely come away empty-handed. In folklore, the hill itself was made from one of the spadefuls of earth thrown up by the devil while he was digging his dyke to drown mankind, and you can still meet him if you run seven times widdershins (anti-clockwise) around the Ring. He will appear and offer you a bowl of soup in return for your soul – a rather poor exchange if you think what he gave Faust.

Six cuckoo superstitions

Whether or not you believe the cuckoo and its unique cry are lucky, both are surrounded with local beliefs.

1. **THE CUCKOO PENNY** – the first time each season you hear the cuckoo call, turn a penny over in your pocket, and you'll never be short of a penny during the following year.

2. **CUCKOO ALE** – When you hear the first cuckoo call, you must go and drink its health immediately at the nearest inn.

3. **CUCKOO COURTING** – Girls waiting for a proposal must count the number of times they hear the cuckoo call; each 'cuckoo' marks a year in the time they must wait to marry.

4. **ROASTED CUCKOO** – a cuckoo roasted in the oven and eaten was believed to relieve sufferers from fits.

5. **IF YOU HEAR THE CUCKOO CALL IN BED**, you will have bad luck unless you remove the sock from your right foot, reciting the rhyme, 'may this to me, lucky be'.

6. **A BABY BORN ON THE DAY THE FIRST CUCKOO CALLS** will be lucky all its life.

☛ *Surely few birds can have carried such a weight of superstitious belief on their shoulders.*

COUNTY ECCENTRICS

'A typical Georgian squire. Larger than life, very generous, very eccentric. And totally sane.'

GEOFF HUTCHINSON, ON 'MAD' JACK FULLER

If the people of Sussex 'wun't be druv', they also often have a broad streak of ECCENTRICITY as well as OBSTINACY in their characters. Down the centuries this has been expressed in a number of ways, some harmless, but some considerably less so.

Mad Jack's pyramid

'MAD' JACK FULLER, the MP for East Sussex and squire of BRIGHTLING (1757-1834), lived life to the full. His 'madness', which nowadays we might consider mere *joie de vivre*, chiefly consisted of the construction of a variety of follies around his estate – among them the BRIGHTLING NEEDLE, which commemorates the English victory at Waterloo, and a pretty and functional observatory designed by the architect SIR ROBERT SMIRKE – but perhaps the maddest was his own mausoleum, a pyramid nearly eight metres high, standing in Brightling's churchyard. Determined to build his own memorial, Fuller completed his tomb 23 years before his death. For many years local lore claimed he had been buried in evening dress, seated upright at a table with a meal and a bottle of port in front of him; sadly, records show that this story is apocryphal, and the interment was carried out in an entirely conventional way.

Sussex mud

It's hard to know whether the author of *A Dictionary of the Sussex Dialect*, the REVEREND WILLIAM PARISH, who published this unexpectedly riveting work in 1875, could really be classed as an eccentric, but anyone who can, straight-faced, classify over 30 different dialect terms for 'MUD' must have a little eccentricity in their character. Here are 17 of the most enticing descriptions:

1. {CLODGY} muddy and wet, like a field path after heavy rain
2. {GAWM} especially sticky, foul-smelling mud
3. {GUBBER} black mud of rotting organic matter
4. {IKE} a mess or area of mud
5. {PUG} a kind of loam, particularly the sticky yellow Wealden clay
6. {SLAB} the thickest mud
7. {SLABBY} sticky, slippery, greasy, dirty mud
8. {SLEECH} mud or river sediment used for manure
9. {SLOB} thick mud
10. {SLOUGH} a muddy hole
11. {SLUB} thick mud (used as 'slush' is elsewhere)
12. {SLURRY} diluted mud, saturated with so much water that it cannot drain
13. {SMEERY} wet and sticky surface mud
14. {STOACH} to trample ground, like cattle, also the silty mud at Rye Harbour
15. {STODGE} thick, puddingy mud
16. {STUG} watery mud
17. {SWANK} a bog

The Inuit are said to have over 40 words to describe snow, but, with mud as their medium, Sussex people run them a close second.

Folklore has it that both the beasts and women of Sussex have unusually long legs – developed through the effort of walking through all that mud.

The Sussex Surrealist

EDWARD JAMES lived in Sussex for much of his youth yet is largely forgotten today. But in the late 1920s and the '30s he was an important patron of the arts. He inherited the large WEST DEAN estate at the age of 25. Condemned as a dilettante by his family, he married the revue dancer Tilly Losch, and began to indulge in the artistic milieu in which he felt at home. He was alleged to be both mean and fastidious – one story said that he would 'boil up a saucepan full of old paperclips drenched in cologne' to reuse them, but there was nothing mean about his patronage. He was close to DALI, and enjoyed the friendship of many artists, particularly the SURREALISTS. At West Dean he had Losch's footprints woven into the stair carpet (after a messy divorce, he replaced it with carpet woven with the pawprint of his favourite wolfhound). Dali designed a sofa in the shape of Mae West's lips for him and he also commissioned the famous lobster telephone.

His portrait was painted by MAGRITTE – but only the back of his head – he's the man in the bowler hat whose rear view we see in *La Reproduction Interdite*. James left England for good in 1940, eventually settling at Xilitla in Mexico, where he created an extraordinary concrete citadel in the jungle, called Las Pozas. He died in 1984, and his body was returned to West Dean for burial.

SAINTS IN SUSSEX

'Father Almighty... now enable me to begin this work...
You have given me the desire to be a builder; make up for my lack of skill.'

PRAYER OF ST CUTHMAN OF STEYNING

Sussex remained a PAGAN LOCATION until well into the eighth century, and many of the saints' legends still told in the county concern those early, itinerant holy men who travelled England preaching the word and founding churches and chapels. Many were on a modest scale, but each represented a few more conversions until, by the ninth century, the country was, nominally at least, fully Christian.

A French visitor

Why ST LEONARD'S FOREST is so named is a mystery – the sixth-century French saint, a nobleman who converted to Christianity at the court of CLOVIS I and subsequently lived as a hermit in the forests of Limousin, seems to have travelled and lived all over Europe. In Sussex he had a job to do – legend says that a fearsome dragon lived in the forest, and the local people called on Leonard to defeat it. When he had successfully banished it, the only reward he asked was that nothing disturb his contemplation – that snakes be banned from the forest, and the nightingales be silenced (their singing had interrupted his meditations). His request is recorded in an ancient couplet about the forest:

'Here the adders never sting,
Nor the nightingales sing'.

How two churches were built

Opposite ST ANDREW'S Church in the village of Steyning sits the statue of a contemplative figure – ST CUTHMAN, looking over the church he is said to have raised in the eighth century. Steyning village sign shows him again, but in a more active pose – pushing his mother in a wheelbarrow. Various stories offer a number of locations for his origin, from Bosham to locations further afield in Devon or even Cornwall, but they agree that he cared for his old mother after the death of his father, living on the charity of others and wheeling her from place to place in a homemade barrow, yoked by a rope around his shoulders. When his first rope broke, he wove a new one from willow stems but fixed with himself that, when the replacement broke, it would be a God-sent sign that he should stop at the spot and raise a church in God's name. The rope broke at Steyning, and Cuthman duly built shelter there for his mother and himself and set to to build a church. The final part of the story is that, towards the end of the building, as he struggled to place a roof beam, a stranger arrived to help him. On Cuthman's asking his name, he answered: '*I am he in whose name you are building this church.*'

An even more eccentric legend surrounds the siting of another church built to St Andrew – this one in Alfriston. This one starts with the arrival of ST ANTHONY at Cuckmere Haven, determined to build a church in the area. Resting in a field, he had a dream that four oxen lay down near him in the shape of a cross, and, taking it as a sign, he built the church on the same spot. Whatever the truth of its origins, the present St Andrew's, dating from the mid-fourteenth century and sometimes called the CATHEDRAL OF THE DOWNS, is a masterpiece – one of those rare churches which has remained unspoiled by any alterations or additions, and most beautifully placed in a slightly elevated position on the village green.

Devil's Dyke

ST CUTHMAN makes another appearance in a story of how Devil's Dyke was formed. The devil is often looked on in Sussex folklore with tolerance and even amusement (there are many tales in which he is easily bested by a shrewd countryman), but in this particular story he plays a suitably demonic part. Sickened by the growth of CHRISTIANITY in Sussex, he decided to dig a channel overnight, flooding the whole county and drowning all his enemies. St Cuthman, hearing of his plan, mimicked dawn, pushing a cockerel off its perch so that it began to crow, while holding a candle behind a sieve to imitate the sunrise. The devil ran off, leaving his dyke only half-dug.

A saint's prayer

A simple prayer, used all over the world, and attributed to ST RICHARD, Bishop of Chichester (1245 and 1253), on his deathbed:

Thanks be to you, my lord, Jesus Christ,
For all the benefits you have given me;
For all the pains and insults you have borne for me.
O, most merciful redeemer, friend and brother,
May I know you more clearly;
Love you more dearly;
And follow you more nearly, day by day.

SUSSEX MARTYRS

'We shall this day light a candle, by God's grace, in England, as I trust shall never been put out.'

BISHOP NICHOLAS RIDLEY, BURNED IN OXFORD, 1555

The story of the SEVENTEEN MARTYRS burned in LEWES is one of the bloodier in Sussex history. The inhumanity of the martyrdoms of the sixteenth century – both CATHOLIC and PROTESTANT, cut deep scars in the country, and a formalised distrust of Catholicism is still expressed in the town every 5 November with the ritualistic burning of the effigy of the pope. That people would be prepared to suffer such a horrible death rather than worship in a church in which the language was not their own seems almost unbelievable today.

The Sussex seventeen

The burning of Protestant believers stepped up during the reign of MARY, a fervent Catholic in the name of her mother Catherine of Aragon, the spurned first wife of HENRY VIII. Lewes, as the county town, was the natural centre for a display that was likely to make the heretics recant, so it was the site of the first burning, of DIRICK CARVER, who had held prayer meetings in his home. His bible was thrown into a barrel on top of a burning bonfire, and he was then pushed into the barrel himself. He threw his bible out into the crowd as he burned, and it is on display in LEWES MUSEUM today. Martyrs were burned on four dates across two years, culminating in a burning of ten people at once, four of them women, in 1557.

The martyrs' memorial

In 1901 a public subscription was got up to build a memorial to the LEWES MARTYRS. Set above the town on the hillside now known as CHAPEL HILL, the obelisk is in a direct line of view from the town hall, site of the martyrdom. The inscription, carefully listing the martyrs' home villages as well as their names, reads:

'In loving memory of the undernamed seventeen Protestant martys who, for faithful testimony to God's truth, were, during the reign of Queen Mary, burned to death in front of the Star Inn – now the Town Hall – Lewes; this obelisk, provided by public subscriptions, was erected A.D. 1901.

Date of Martyrdom, July 22nd, 1555 † *DIRICK CARVER, of Brighton. Date of Martyrdom, June 6th, 1555 † THOMAS HARLAND and † JOHN OSWALD, both of Woodmancote. † THOMAS AVINGTON and † THOMAS REED, both of Ardingly. Date of Martyrdom, about June 20th, 1556. † THOMAS WOOD (a minister of the Gospel) of Lewes. † THOMAS MYLES, of Hellingly. Date of Martyrdome, June 22nd, 1557. † RICHARD WOODMAN and † GEORGE STEVENS, both of Warbleton. † ALEXANDER HOSMAN, † WILLIAM MAINARD, and † THOMASINA WOOD, all of Mayfield. † MARGERY MORRIS and † JAMES MORRIS (her son) both of Heathfield. † DENIS BURGES, of Buxted. † ANN ASHTON, of Rotherfield. † MARY GROVES, of Lewes.*

'And they overcame because of the blood of the Lamb; and because of the word of their testimony; and they loved not their live even unto death.'

REV. XII, 11, R.V.

John Foxe's testimony

FOXE, a long-time Protestant and sympathiser with the Protestant cause, produced what is now popularly known as FOXE'S MARTYRS, in association with JOHN DAY, a printer, in 1563. Its first full title was *Actes and Monuments of these latter and perilous Dayes, touching matters of the Church, wherein are comprehended and described the great Persecution and horrible Troubles that have been wrought and practised by the Romish Prelates, especiallye in this Realme of England and Scotland, from the yeare of our Lorde a thousande to the time now present. Gathered and collected according to the true Copies and Wrytinges certificatorie as well of the Parties themselves that Suffered, as also out of die Biship's Registers, which were the Doers thereof, by John Foxe*. Little wonder that it acquired a short title, too, although the eighteen hundred pages that followed did exactly what was claimed on the tin.

Foxe left us the only record of three martyrs burned at GRENESTEDE (now East Grinstead); nothing else is known of them.

'Near about the same tyme... suffered other three likewise at Grenested in Sussex, two men and one woman, the names of whom were Tho. Dungage, Iohn Forman, and mother Tree, who for rightousnes sake, gave them selves to death and tormentes of the fire, paciently abidyng what the furious rage of man could say or worke agaynst them, at the sayd Towne of Grenested endying their lives, the xviij. of the sayd moneth of Iuly, and in the yeare aforesayd [1556]'

CHAPTER THREE

HISTORICAL SUSSEX

Every county has the same amount of history, of course, but the visitor could be forgiven for thinking that Sussex has more than most. Studded with manmade evidence of a busy past, every hill seems to have its grand house or castle, every hamlet its church, and every graveyard seems to be literally stuffed with the memorably worded memorials of people who have left their mark. The famously muddy roads of the county for a long time kept even its own communities rather separate and self-contained, so it is noticeable that the tales and lore of Sussex tend towards a particularly local note – the slow rate at which news travelled in times past is illustrated by the tale of the Sussex farmer who, requested during the Civil War to clear his fields to allow representatives of the two sides to skirmish, looked on, scratched his head, and remarked 'they've come to blows then?' – this in 1645, nearly three years after the conflict had started.

After serious transport arrived in Sussex – and that really meant with the advent of the railway lines in the first half of the nineteenth century – the local history begins to weave into slightly thicker strands, and to become a little more generic. Although the image of Sussex's backwardness persisted well into the twentieth century, by the time Chichester and Brighton were both within easy travelling distance of London this perception was giving way and long before it had faded altogether visitors were already arriving in ever-greater numbers, drawn equally by the popular pleasures of the seaside and the more high-minded attractions of those historical artefacts which so generously litter the Sussex landscape.

SUSSEX CASTLES

'We wish our readers to go to Petworth... where they will find the coolest grottoes and the finest Vandykes in the world.'

WILLIAM HAZLITT, *SKETCHES OF THE PRINCIPAL PICTURE GALLERIES IN ENGLAND*, 1824

With a long history of coastal defence and plenty of FEUDAL LORDS, Sussex has plenty of CASTLES. ARUNDEL is perhaps the most impressive, BODIAM, floating on its broad moat, the most magical – and there are dozens of ruins that could, today, lay title to the most minimal – but wherever you go in the county a castle of some sort, even a ruined one, will never be far away.

Why Norfolk?

One might well ask why the DUKES OF NORFOLK own ARUNDEL CASTLE. As usual with ancient English sites, the answer lies in an alliance by marriage. After the family of its builder was banished abroad, the castle was at various times owned by the Crown, and was first gifted to the D'ALBINI family, then passed through the female line to the FITZALANS, made Earls of Arundel. The Fitzalan male line died with the twelfth Earl and his daughter inherited the castle. She married THOMAS HOWARD, fourth Duke of Norfolk, and the castle and its lands have remained with the Dukes of Norfolk ever since.

CASTLE ILLUMINATIONS

Electricity was installed in Arundel Castle in the 1890s, at the then-immense cost of £36,000.

The ghosts of Arundel Castle

The most complete of Sussex's castles, ARUNDEL might also be able to make a claim to be the most haunted.

Between four and seven ghosts are regular visitors, depending on whose account you read. Two definite presences are those of the BLUE MAN, who appears harmlessly browsing the library, dressed in clothes from the Royalist period, and the mistreated scullion, a little BOY, beaten to death at some unknown date, who scuttles about the kitchen sweeping and scouring, as he did in life.

By far the most sinister legend is that of the WHITE BIRD – some versions cite a white owl – which appears fluttering at the windows when a member of the incumbent family is about to die.

Bramber versus Arundel

It seems strange that two castles arising from such similar origins should have met such different fates, one a ruined fragment, the other a vast and elaborate triumph.

- BRAMBER was built in around 1070 by William De Braose, a friend of William the Conqueror.
- ARUNDEL was built by Roger de Montgomery, a trusted friend of William the Conqueror after he was given the rape (district) of Arundel in 1067.

Both castles originally followed the motte and bailey pattern characteristic of those built in the eleventh century.

- BRAMBER remained in the ownership of the De Braose family until they died out in 1324. Subsequently it was allowed to fall into disrepair, and gradually fell from historical accounts. Now only a part of the gatehouse survives, jutting poignantly up from its elevated site like a single tooth.
- ARUNDEL, on the other hand, was lived in and augmented, century by century. Although it endured two sieges during the Civil War – once by Cavaliers and once by Roundheads, it remained in ruins for some decades, but the eleventh Duke of Norfolk renovated it at the end of the eighteenth century. The last of subsequent additions and restorations was completed in 1906. Today it is one of the most magnificent castles remaining in the south of England.

The castle that never was

The YPRES TOWER still stands in Rye, now part of the town museum, and was long thought to have been part of an ancient castle there. Certainly there were plans to build a castle in the time of Henry III – the early thirteenth century – but there is no evidence that one was ever built there. This has not deterred the *Ypres Castle Inn*, a seventeenth-century pub just in the shadow of the tower, from displaying a full medieval castle on its hanging sign.

Six other Sussex castles

- AMBERLEY – Founded in 1103.
- CAMBER – An ancient site, now ruined.
- HASTINGS – Founded in 1070.
- HERSTMONCEUX – Built in the fifteenth century.
- LEWES – An ancient and much altered site.
- PEVENSEY – A fortress since Roman times.

BODIAM CASTLE
& ERIC THE SLENDER

This tantalising entry appears in the British Film Index. Produced in 1926, it was a two-reel silent movie in a series that appears to have focused on castles of Britain and their ghosts. Regrettably there is no way in which it can be procured for viewing today, so its content can only be a matter of speculation!

BATTLES & CONFLICTS

'There were killed King Harold, and Earl Leofwine his brother, and Earl Gyrth his brother, and many good men.'

THE ANGLO-SAXON CHRONICLE, ACCOUNT OF THE BATTLE OF HASTINGS

With few large towns and a largely agricultural make up, Sussex has not played a very major part in countrywide conflict since the NORMAN INVASION. Nonetheless, she has supplied plenty of SOLDIERS to fight away from home, and her history can offer a few military aspects, even within the county.

Three Sussex battles

Sussex has been the site of relatively few BATTLES. Nonetheless, here are two that made an impact well beyond the borders of the country, and one less important skirmish that was later honoured with the title of 'battle':

1. **THE BATTLE OF HASTINGS**
14 October, 1066
(Actually fought at present-day Battle)
PROTAGONISTS: King Harold of England and William, Duke of Normandy
OUTCOME: The Norman invasion became the Norman conquest.

2. **THE BATTLE OF LEWES**
12-14 May, 1264
PROTAGONISTS: King Edward III of England and Simon de Montfort, Earl of Leicester
OUTCOME: De Montfort upheld the cause against increasing Royal tyranny, but was killed at the Battle of Evesham in 1265. Nevertheless, he had established principles which were to underpin the development of modern DEMOCRATIC GOVERNMENT.

And the small battle, seldom heard of, is

3. **THE BATTLE OF HAYWARDS HEATH**
November 1642
PROTAGONISTS: Sir Edward Ford, Royalist, and a part of the Parliamentarian forces
OUTCOME: The Royalists were forced to abandon their attempt to seize the town of Lewes. A little-known chapter in the Civil War, spilling over into a county that was far from the most active in those turbulent years.

The Royal Sussex Regiment

MOTTO: *Nothing Succeeds like Sussex*
REGIMENTAL MARCH: *John Baines' Regimental Marches*
AFFECTIONATELY KNOWN AS: *The Haddocks, The Iron Regiment, The Orange Lilies*

The Sussex was founded in 1881, formed from the 35th Regiment of Foot (the Royal Sussex) and the 107th Regiment of Foot (the Bengal Light Infantry).

It had two battalions, the first of which spent WORLD WAR I at the North West Frontier, while the second fought in the trenches in France.

The regiment served between 1861 and 1966. Its worst moment came on 30 June 1916 in France, which afterwards became known as 'the Day Sussex died'; 17 officers and 349 men were killed and a further thousand wounded or taken prisoner. Nonetheless, the regiment survived to serve in WORLD WAR II.

The legacy of Duke William

Grace in victory does not seem to have been one of the CONQUEROR's qualities. Not only was the location of the Saxons' defeat to be marked by a great commemorative abbey, but WILLIAM decreed that the altar of the abbey church should be built on the exact spot where KING HAROLD fell. The abbey was destroyed during HENRY VIII's dissolution, but a stone still marks the spot where Harold died and where the high altar stood.

A woman soldier

Words on a stone found in the graveyard of ST NICHOLAS' CHURCH in Brighton:

'IN MEMORY OF
PHOEBE HESSEL
who was born at Stepney in
the Year 1713 She served for
many Years as a private soldier in
the 5th Reg. of foot in different parts
of Europe and in the year 1745 fought
under the command of the DUKE OF
CUMBERLAND at the Battle of Fontenoy
where she received a Bayonet wound in
her Arm Her long life which commenced
in the time of QUEEN ANNE extended
to the reign of GEORGE IV by whose
munificence she received comfort and
support in her latter years she died
at Brighton where she had long
resided December 12th 1821
Aged 108 Years'

Quite a life – although many thought PHOEBE HESSEL had usefully embroidered on it in old age. As remarkable as her military history is the fact that she worked as a street vendor – selling fish and vegetables – in Brighton until well into her nineties.

GARDENS & GARDENING

'Annihilating all that's made
To a green thought in a green shade'

ANDREW MARVELL, *THE GARDEN*

ACID and ALKALINE, CHALK and CLAY, the soil of Sussex, allied with a gentle and plant-friendly climate, can be kind to GARDENERS provided that they are prepared to work with the raw materials nature has handed them. There's the potential for most kinds of garden here, although not all in the same part of the county. For the visitor, though, Sussex offers a positive embarrassment of riches.

Five Sussex gardens owned by writers and artists

Many creative people have made their homes in Sussex, and many have also made wonderful gardens there. Here are five that can be visited, although all their makers are now gone.

1. **LAMB HOUSE**, *Rye*
Not perhaps Sussex's most notable garden, but one in which the visitor can imagine E. F. BENSON and HENRY JAMES strolling together in the early years of the twentieth century – and literary gardens don't come much more prestigious than that.

2. **BATEMANS**, *Burwash*
KIPLING's garden, and one that seems to encapsulate English country life at its gentlest and most productive, with separate areas for a formal garden, an orchard, a kitchen-garden, a rose garden, and a number of other 'outside rooms' against the backdrop of a beautiful and historic house.

3. **CHARLESTON**, *Firle*
The famous garden of Sussex's two 'Bloomsbury options'. Although the garden at Charleston is humble in scale most of those members of the BLOOMSBURY GROUP who were habitués of the house lifted a trowel in it at one time or another; it remains a very personal space. The terrace – known to its familiars as the piazza – has a mosaic of broken crockery and a small fountain lined by tiles made by QUENTIN BELL.

4. **MONKS HOUSE**, *Rodmell*
Monks House (traditionally it is spelled without an apostrophe), is small and simple – but its garden is surprisingly large. The second garden in Sussex that might be said to be characteristically 'Bloomsbury', it was the great love and occupation of LEONARD WOOLF, who made it into a productive and happy space, with

greenhouses, beehives and an orchard, as well as a well-stocked and devotedly tended vegetable garden.

And, last but not least, a garden created by someone who was great in both fields, but who was very definitely a gardener first:

5. **Great Dixter**, *Northiam*

Christopher Lloyd was famous as a gardener and plantsman first and an author second – this is not to downplay his role as a writer, but reflects the fact that he lived and breathed gardens. He died in 2006, and his exciting garden at Great Dixter serves as a fitting legacy to him.

Making a Sussex trug

What's a Trug? A trug is a traditional shallow, oval, handled basket originally used as a measure around the farm, but long since appropriated for use in the garden, for weeding, planting, carrying fruit, flowers and vegetables and a host of other tasks. Trugs have been traditional 'carriers' in Sussex for at least two centuries and probably longer.

How is it made?

The slatted boards that are curved to make the sides and ends of the trug are made from willow, and the thicker handle and rim from chestnut. A cleaving axe (an axe with a relatively thin blade) is used to split the strips from the chestnut, and handle and rim are then bent around a former to make their shape.

The willow boards are smoothed before being soaked. While still wet, they are fitted into the frame and nailed in place. When dry, the basket has a solid base that will give many years' good service.

A warmer Sussex?

Many are agreed that England must have been warmer in Roman times.

The great Roman villa at Fishbourne would have been surrounded by extensive gardens, and records survive of the Roman gardeners bringing figs, peaches, almonds and grapes, and growing them successfully. The mild climate of Sussex is as good as any in England for such experiments, but it would be a confident gardener today who attempted to grow almonds.

The hottest chilli

It seems fitting that the gardens of West Dean, home of the British Surrealist Edward James, holds one of the exotic events in the Sussex calendar – a chilli-growers festival – every August. It offers plants and seed of different chilli types from all over the world, and the opportunity to burn your mouth in a range of different heat units, from the relatively mild jalapeno with a Scoville heat rating of between 2,500 and 5000 all the way up to the very hottest habaneros (the hottest chilli on record is the *Red Savina Habanero*, with a heat rating of 570,000 Scoville units).

MONUMENTS & GRAVESTONES

'Steel True, Blade Straight'

EPITAPH ON THE GRAVESTONE OF SIR ARTHUR CONAN DOYLE,
ORIGINALLY IN THE WINDLESHAM ESTATE

There's not enough space here to do full justice to the MONUMENTS and GRAVESTONES of Sussex – the county, East and West, has more memorable EPITAPHS and EFFIGIES than most, and even visitors who aren't normally engaged by these messages from the past will find the stones in many of the county's older graveyards are entertaining and often educational.

A lost technique

At the end of the eighteenth century a potter, JONATHAN HARMER, son of the Heathfield stonemason, introduced a novelty line in gravestone decoration – glazed terracotta plaques set directly into the stones. He offered a range of designs – urns, cherubs, a melancholic mother and child in languishing pose, and (most popular) a bowl of fruit and flowers. They were inset into carved indentations in gravestones, and mortared in place, although exactly how was never recorded. They were quickly taken up by well-to-do Sussex, and for twenty years Harmer did a brisk trade in his stones. The surprising thing today is their longevity; terracotta might not be expected to prove particularly hardy exposed to the elements, but, two hundred years after they were set up, many examples are still in excellent condition. Harmer never passed on the secrets of their manufacture and when he died in 1839 the brief fashion died with him. Surviving Harmer stones can be still be seen in the church-yards of, among others, Salehurst, Burwash, East Hoathly, Herstmonceux and Glynde.

A writer's epitaph

One of the saddest memorials in Sussex is that erected to the writer VIRGINIA WOOLF in the garden of her last home, MONKS HOUSE in Rodmell, near where her ashes had been scattered under a pair of elm trees. It is simply carved with a quotation from her novel *The Waves*, and a portrait bust sculpted by STEPHEN TOMLIN sits on the flint wall above it:

> *'"Death is the enemy. Against you*
> *I will fling myself unvanquished*
> *and unyielding – O Death!"*
> *The waves broke on the shore'*

The Chattri

At first glance, the CHATTRI, situated high on the Sussex Downs at Patcham, looking out over the landscape below, recalls an oriental folly, perhaps built by some contemporary of the Prince Regent's, with its cultural echo of the Pavilion at Brighton. Actually it was erected more than a full century later, in 1921, to commemorate 53 of the Sikh and Hindu soldiers who fought in World War I and who died in the hospitals of Sussex. The word 'chattri' means UMBRELLA, and reflects the domed roof of the elegant little pavilion. It marks the spot where, in keeping with their faith, the soldiers' bodies were cremated, and commands a particularly beautiful view, though hardly one that recalls the homeland of the dead.

The heart of a crusader

Visitors to the church of ST GILES in Horsted Keynes may wonder at the diminutive size of the crusader laid out on his tomb there. Well under a metre long, the tomb is otherwise conventional for a knight who had fought for his faith in the HOLY LAND – the figure's mailed feet rest on a crouching lion, and his hands are laid peacefully on his breast. The explanation is that this is probably the memorial to a heart burial; when crusaders were killed in remote lands, their bodies were sometimes buried where they died, but their hearts were returned to their home to be interred by their family. This little knight is probably guarding the casket which contains only his heart.

A WOODEN MEMORIAL

Early wooden tomb sculptures survive only rarely – they're too vulnerable to rot, worm and other enemies. The twelfth-century church at Slindon, though, has an effigy dating from 1539. It is carved from oak, is just over 5ft long, and depicts Sir Anthony St Leger in the formal and elaborate clothing of the mid-sixteenth century, with a careful attention to detail, including sleeve pleating and an impressive codpiece.

SUSSEX HOUSES

'Years ago I had a house in Sussex. It was like Arcadia, with an old Victorian bridge, a pond and the Downs'

NICOLAS ROEG, FILM DIRECTOR

The houses of Sussex have plenty of character, whether they're COTTAGES in remote villages, MOATED MANSIONS in large grounds, or TRADESMEN'S DWELLING in the old county towns. And plenty of old houses remain – towns such as Lewes have never suffered large-scale demolition at their centres, and the more rural parts of Sussex were remote until relatively recently, so have never become so much of a 'suburb' as the county's proximity to London might suggest.

Six houses to visit in Sussex

Sussex is full of HOUSES that merit a visit; the list below covers some – more or less known – not mentioned elsewhere in the miscellany. Some may be visited by appointment only.

1. **FARLEY FARM**, *Chiddingly*
The home of the photographer and artist's muse LEE MILLER, who lived here with her second husband, the art historian ROLAND PENROSE. Not only does the farmhouse contain many works by the couple's friends, PICASSO, MAN RAY and MAX ERNST among them, but it is also full of memorabilia from Miller's fascinating pre-Sussex life.

2. **FIRLE PLACE**, *Firle*
A strange chateau-like façade was added to an older house in the eighteenth century, built from Caen stone, unusual in such a flint-led district, but probably taken from the ruins of a local monastery after the dissolution.

3. **NEWTIMBER PLACE**, *Hassocks*
An attractive sixteenth-century house held within a broad moat, with a flint and brick façade and a roof tiled with Horsham stone – an extraordinarily heavy medium that is deemed too impractical to use today. The hall is lined with 'Etruscan-style' murals painted in the eighteenth century.

4. **PETWORTH HOUSE**, *Petworth*
A well-known National Trust treasure with an in-house gallery that contains

many great works by artists including TITIAN, TURNER, BLAKE, GAINSBOROUGH, REYNOLDS and VAN DYCK. The property of the Earls of Northumberland since the twelfth century, the house sits in grounds designed by CAPABILITY BROWN.

5. **SAINT HILL MANOR,** *East Grinstead*
A list of its owners is almost as interesting as the house itself. Its final owner, the founder of the Church of Scientology, L.RON HUBBARD, bought it from the MAHARAJAH OF JAIPUR; earlier caretakers included American hostess MRS DREXREL BIDDLE, who commissioned the house's monkey mural. Painted by JOHN SPENCER CHURCHILL (a nephew of Winston), it depicts twenty different kinds of monkey engaged in human activities (Sir Winston himself is shown as a venerable capuchin monkey at his easel).

6. **ST MARY'S HOUSE,** *Bramber*
Originally built in 1470 by the BISHOP OF WINCHESTER as a monastic inn for pilgrims, this fine fifteenth-century house is frequently used as a setting for film and television drama, and is one of few houses in England to have original panelling made from gilded and painted leather.

The building materials of Sussex

No-one is so to-the-point on this subject as NIKOLAUS PEVSNER; the Sussex volume (written with Ian Nairn) from the classic *Buildings of England* series, notes:

'Flint on the Downs and the coastal plain... Sandstone in the Weald itself, usually buff-coloured from Horsham eastwards, nutty and brown in the hills around Pulborough, greenish in the NW corner, N of Midhurst, where it is the same as the Burgate stone of Surrey. And after that, of course, brick everywhere; first seen at Herstmonceux Castle in the mid C15, now over the whole county, usually a cheerful vermilion. Brighton and Lewes (E), different as usual, developed their black-glazed bricks for a few years at the end of the C18 and then, sadly, abandoned them in favour of stucco.'

Neat, concise and memorable.

Moving house

One of the most remarkable things about the WEALD AND DOWNLAND OPEN AIR MUSEUM at Singleton is that every building on the site has been moved from somewhere else – and although they are all Sussex houses now, by dint of their location, some started life in Kent, Surrey or Hampshire. Just four of the most interesting reconstructed dwellings and other secular buildings:

TOLL COTTAGE, *1807* – from Beeding, Sussex

MARKET HALL, *1620* – from Titchfield, Hampshire

MEDIEVAL SHOP – from Horsham, Sussex

FLINT-AND-BRICK HOUSE, *medieval-seventeenth century* – from Walderton, Sussex.

SUSSEX CHURCHES

'The effect is unforgettable: the plain like a sea… punctuated by only one slim spire'

IAN NAIRN, (OF CHICHESTER CATHEDRAL), *THE BUILDINGS OF ENGLAND: SUSSEX*

Although Sussex can only boast one CATHEDRAL, in CHICHESTER, a 1911 survey claims over 400 churches for the county, many very ancient and some very small. Before better roads arrived in the late nineteenth century, churches were often built to serve remote farming communities and parishes with relatively small numbers of people, and these VILLAGE CHURCHES offer the visitor a great variety of idiosyncratic features.

The devil's exit

When a child is baptised, the evil leaves its soul – and Sussex wisdom has it that, since the DEVIL has to escape by some means, he must leave by the north door, often known as 'THE DEVIL'S DOOR'. In some churches the north door was only ever opened during a baptism. Well over forty Sussex churches have a blocked north door 'to keep the Devil out' , and some of the blocked doors are so tiny that they can have had only a symbolic use. How the Devil is expected to escape, however, when his door has been walled up goes unrecorded. Churches where you can still clearly see the Devil's blocked door can be found at the following locations, to name but a few:

• Birdham • Ditchling
• Folkington • Hamsey
• Hangleton • Lullington
• Milland Old Chapel, East Chiltington
• Patcham • Piddinghoe
• Selmeston • Sompting

The Hardham anchorite

In the thirteenth century Sussex had many ANCHORITES – men and women who had themselves immured for life in tiny cells attached to churches, with the purpose of praying for the living outside their walls. St Richard of Chichester made a number of bequests to specific anchorites over his life and in his will in 1253. One such was at Hardham where a wattle-and-daub structure eight feet square is recorded, with a 'narrow and convenient' window through which his food could be passed, and at which people could seek counsel with him. THE HARDHAM 'ANKER' would have served a year's probation before being locked up for life in his insecure cell; to the modern mind the prospect might seem hideous, but he was at least guaranteed a roof and food. One thirteenth-century document refers to them 'living under the eaves of the church, like the night fowl'.

Records of anchorites at some other Sussex churches:

- † **St John's Sub Castro** (Lewes): a Dane 'of noble birth' named Magnus.
- † **Chichester Cathedral:** Father William Bolle, originally rector of Aldrington.
- † **Steyning:** a woman called Miliana, who brought lawsuits from her cell – first against the Hardham anchorite then against the Hardham prior, for money and goods she was allegedly owed.
- † plus unnamed men at **Stedham**, **Pagham** and **Findon**, and women at **St Anne's** in **Lewes**, **Houghton** and **Stopham**.

Some Sussex rarities

Sussex has only three churches with round towers:

- † **St Michael's**, Lewes; Pevsner says the church is 'assigned to C13, a puzzlingly late date'.
- † **St John the Evangelist**, Piddinghoe, early twelfth century.
- † **Southease Parish Church**, Saxon, date unknown.

There are only 181 of these round towers in the whole of England, and all but six are in East Anglia. The areas in which they were built have no building stone, only flint, so it was easier for the builders to execute a curve than to make square corners.

The smallest church

LULLINGTON lays claim to having the smallest church in the county – and, at 16ft (5m) square, it is certainly compact. It seats twenty at a pinch, and is all that remains of a bigger building – a medieval church, of which this is the chancel. Diminutive as it is, it can still boast a belfry and spire, an altar, font and lectern.

ROME COMES TO GORING-BY-SEA

The Church of the English Martyrs in Goring-by-Sea offers a most unusual attraction: the only known reproduction of Michelangelo's Sistine Chapel Ceiling in the world. The ceiling is scaled at two-thirds of the original, and was painted by Gary Bevans, a signpainter without formal art training, who was inspired to start the work after a parish pilgrimage to Rome.

TRANSPORT IN SUSSEX

'The Siddlesham snail, the Siddlesham snail,
The boiler's bust, she's off the rail'

ANONYMOUS DOGGEREL DECRYING THE – NOW DEFUNCT – SELSEY TRAIN

It seems odd now, with the FAST TRAIN FROM BRIGHTON to the terminal at VICTORIA taking well under an hour, and more than its fair share of motorways crossing the county, that Sussex should have been considered until well into the nineteenth century as a remote and rather inturned place. The famous mud, in all its depth and clagginess, is mentioned by authors from Defoe onwards as a good reason not to travel, so the coming of the RAILWAY made a huge difference – both to the wider world's perception of Sussex in general, and to Sussex's view of 'foreigners' (previously a term for anyone from further away than the next village) in particular.

A practical and a writer's view

The success of the London-to-Manchester railway prompted a group of businessmen to put up the money for a London-to-Brighton link. By the 1830s Brighton was attracting more than 2,000 visitors a week, so there was no question of the level of the

demand. A proposal by GEORGE RENNIE for the proposed route was eventually accepted, and the railway was begun in 1838 and completed in 1841. A handful of facts and figures:

AMOUNT OF NEW TRACK: *39 miles*

LENGTH OF NEW TUNNELS:

Balcombe – *800 yards*
Clayton Hill – *1,730 yards*
Haywards Heath – *1,450 yards*
Merstham – *2,180 yards*

COST OF THE RAILWAY:
£2,634,059.00 (or *£57,262 per mile*)

COST OF TICKETS ON OPENING:

First class *14s 6d* (an immense sum in the 1840s)

Second class *9s 6d*

Third class *6s* (travelling in some discomfort; the third-class carriages were open to the elements)

KIPLING was a keen railway traveller and in 1900 produced a piece of whimsy about the building of the southern coast railways, written in the style of the ARABIAN NIGHTS: '... A certain Afrit of little sense and great power... who had devised brazen engines that ran on iron roads. These by the perfection of their operation, dilated the heart with wonder and the eye with amazement, for they resembled, as it were, litters drawn by fire-breathing dragons...' The places linked in the story have been renamed, but it does not take much thought to identify them – try Tabriziz, Harundil and Isbahan.*

*Three Bridges, Arundel & Eastbourne

Odd conveyances

LICENCES to park are nothing new; they've been with us since long before the coming of the motor car. Eastbourne boasts a number of Victorian licences still on display, in the form of small initialled iron plates inserted into the older walls of the town at street level. They specify the form of conveyance they licence by means of initials:

BCS . . . . *Bath chair stand*
GCS . . . . *Goat chaise stand*
HCS . . . . *Hackney carriage stand*
LPS . . . . *Luggage porter stand*
MCS . . . . *Motor charabanc stand*
SDS . . . . *Saddled donkey stand*
SPS . . . . *Saddled pony stand*

Balcombe viaduct

Originally built to take the London to Brighton railway over the River Ouse, the BALCOMBE VIADUCT has been lauded ever since its opening as one of the most elegant in Britain.

A plaque on one arch gives the reader all the salient points:

'BALCOMBE
Ouse Valley Viaduct

This viaduct was designed by the engineer John Urpeth Rastrick for the London & Brighton Railway. The architect David Mocatta was associated with the design.

The structure comprises thirty-seven arches and was completed in 1842. It is listed Grade II Restored 1996-99'

To which one could add that the viaduct is 1,475ft long, and 96ft about the ground at its highest point. The bricks fused to build it were brought from Holland and transported by boat up the – then much wider and deeper – Ouse. The view from the viaduct through the train windows is lovely, and the view of the viaduct from the fields below is breathtaking.

CHAPTER FOUR

SUSSEX SUSTENANCE

The famously firm and obstinate people of Sussex are strengthened by more than mere food and drink – although both are important in the county's life, and there are numerous specialities to be had, of a varying deliciousness, from Sussex perry to the ubiquitous Sussex puddings. The fare was obviously sustaining, even if a century or two ago many early versions of those puddings were made from little more than plain suet and flour – because the society it produced flourished at many levels. Never a poor county, with agriculture, fishing and hunting plenteous, Sussex hasn't ever left her sturdy natives to go hungry, and her children are 'good do'ers' (an expression taken from Parish's notes on Sussex dialect – meaning anything from a hen to a child that thrives without much trouble taken).

Beyond the diet, sustenance is found in the wide and generous society – even Defoe was impressed by the open-handed Sussex people, although he deplored the condition of their roads.

Social equality seems to have been found early on here – perhaps fostered by the independent mind for which the Sussex native is known – so that hunting parsons, shepherds, fishermen, and milkmaids all rubbed shoulders together without much dissent.

SUSSEX KITCHENS

'A surgeon may as well attempt to open a vein with an oyster knife, as for me to pretend to get dinner without proper tools to do it...'

WILLIAM VERRAL, MASTER OF THE WHITE HART INN, LEWES, 1759

The COOKS in Sussex, as in many other primarily agricultural counties, were excellent managers. To be 'nottable', a dialect word meaning thrifty, was a much-praised quality in the kitchen. Flour and suet eked out scanty supplies of meat, and the cheaper fish – such as mackerel and herring – cooked in various ways were also staples in SUSSEX KITCHENS. Numerous recipes from these more economical times still exist, although many may not sound enormously appealing to today's more indulged palates.

Five cheap Sussex dinners

1. TEN-TO-ONE PIE
Potato and meat pie (ten potatoes to each piece of meat).
2. SWIMMERS
Plain suet pudding cut in slices and sweetened with jam or treacle.
3. SUSSEX PUDDING
A plain pudding made with flour and water. Also sometimes less genteelly known as 'hard dick', 'hard' used in the sense of plain or mean. A less pinchpenny version was made with raisins ('spotted dick'). Quite a different matter from Sussex Pond Pudding (*see p61*).
4. BLOCK ORNAMENTS
Cheap offcuts of every kind of meat, bought by the handful or bag from the butcher, and scattered lightly across the ubiquitous suet crust to make a 'meat' pudding.
5. SHACKLE
Watery soup made with vegetables.

...And to wash them down:

DONKEY TEA
Toasted breadcrumbs in water, strained and sweetened with sugar.

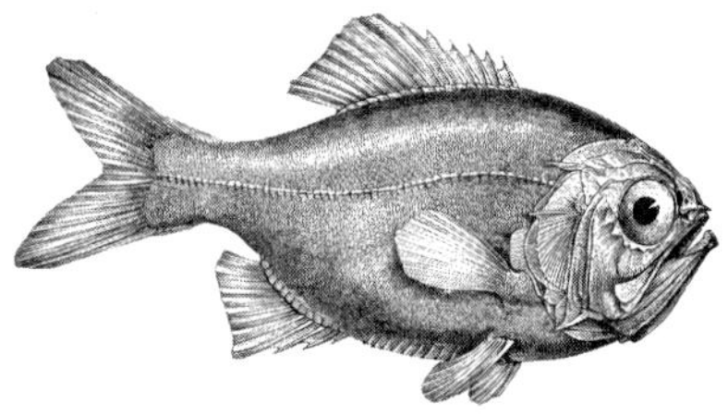

Fish suppers

HERRINGS, MACKEREL, SPRATS and SARDINES were the cheap fish that formed the standby of the thrifty Sussex cook. Local recipes (some so local as to be specific to a single village or town) were passed down through families. Selsey herrings were herrings soused in vinegar accompanied by a fresh horseradish sauce, but other richer recipes exist featuring cream and pastry.

The Sussex coastline, even in these over-fished times, still offers rich pickings for catch-your-own enthusiasts. Fishermen's records show that the following species were line-caught on the stretch of coast between West Wittering and Selsey Bill between 2003 and 2006:

Bream *(including Gilthead Bream)* . . .
Codling . . . .
Dogfish . . . .
Flounder . . . .
Gurnard . . . .
Huss . . . .
Mackerel . . . .
Mullet . . . .
Plaice . . . .
Pouting . . . .
Ray . . . .
Sole . . . .
Whiting . . . .

The seven good things

A Chichester lobster,
a Selsey cockle,
An Arundel mullet,
a Pulborough eel,
An Amberley trout,
a Rye herring
And a Bourne wheatear,
are the best of their kind

This is a TRADITIONAL RHYME lauding the finest raw ingredients of the country. The wheatear (a sparrow-sized bird) was rarely eaten by the beginning of the twentieth century (and there aren't reliable records of it being eaten before then, but rooks, blackbirds and sparrows all featured in pies in the nineteenth century). All the other edibles, though, remain possibilities. In 2003, a television programme made by BBC South East undertook to provide a recipe for each of the seven good things, but even they jibbed at the wheatear.

PUDDING PEOPLE

Sussex was so well known for the ubiquity of its puddings – some form or other of which appeared at every meal – that the saying arose, 'Don't go to Sussex, or they'll make you into a pudding.'

LOCAL SPECIALITIES

'Eat winkles in March;
they're as good as a dose of medicine'

TRADITIONAL SUSSEX SAYING

From the time of the Romans – who no doubt enjoyed lavish villa meals of DORMICE IN HONEY in Sussex, as they did in many other parts of Britain – the county has been home to a wide variety of foods and cooking. From the traditional pies and puddings and the indigenous meat, fish and game, to the lavish creations of cooks who learned their arts in foreign cities, SUSSEX FOOD has long enjoyed a fine reputation.

Twelve exotic dishes of William Verral

The following twelve exotic dishes were listed, among many others equally appetising, as his specialities in the 1759 cookbook of WILLIAM VERRAL, celebrated Francophile chef of the WHITE HART INN in Lewes (the spelling is from the original):

1. *Water souchy* (a delicate fish soup)
2. *Cups of eggs with gravy of partridge*
3. *Petty-pattees in cups. With a Benjamele sauce.*
4. *Sheeps rumps fry'd*
5. *Pigeons au soleil*
6. *Cardoons, with piquant sauce*
7. *Fricasee of eels, with Champagne or Rhenish wine*
8. *Small fat pig en balon. Sauce in ravigote*
9. *Calves ears, with lettuce*
10. *Truffles in French wine*
11. *Cups a l'amande, with sweet biscuit*
12. *Currant fritters en surprize*

Some of these sound more palatable than others (sheeps' rumps, however well fried, would probably appeal to few people today), but surely the White Hart menus must have been some of the most sophisticated in eighteenth-century Sussex. Verral had trained under M. DE SAINT CLOUET, a famous French cook of the time.

THE PRICE OF A MEAL

In 1768, an elaborate electioneering dinner for 145 people at the White Hart Inn cost twenty-one pounds and fifteen shillings. The drinks bill came to over three times as much.

A true local pudding

One dish universally acclaimed as indigenous to Sussex is the SUSSEX POND PUDDING. Boiled in a cloth, this looks like any other suet pudding until you cut into it, whereupon it releases a flood of lemon-flavoured sauce (the 'pond'). The secret to the recipe is that a whole lemon is placed in the suet casing, along with generous quantities of butter and brown sugar. The lemon softens in the three- or four-hour boiling of the pudding, and each serving contains a slice of the succulent fruit. Although enthusiasts claim an ancient history for the recipe, lemons would not have been available in Sussex, even to the moneyed gentry, until the early nineteenth century, so it is probably no more than two hundred years old.

A fatal event

The Sussex oyster industry took its final blow in 1902, when EMSWORTH OYSTERS were served at a banquet held by the local mayor. Unfortunately the shellfish beds had been contaminated by the relaying of local drains alongside them, and several of the guests contracted typhoid. There were a number of fatalities, including the Dean of Winchester, and appetite for the local oysters died with the victims.

Sussex oysters

The ROMANS enjoyed the fine quality of Sussex fish, and particularly the LOCAL OYSTERS – copious quantities of oyster shells were found, amongst other food detritus, in the ruins of the palatial Roman villa at Fishbourne. And future generations followed their lead. By the nineteenth century, SHOREHAM was one of the most successful fishing ports in Sussex, and a centre of the county's oyster trade.

Here are some statistics relating to Sussex's oyster trade:

[295] the number of boats fishing out of Shoreham in 1869

[740] the number of men employed on the boats

[89] the number of boys employed on the boats

[20,000] the number of oysters sent up from Shoreham to London per annum (several times this number were consumed locally).

☛ *The mid-1800s were the heyday of Sussex fisheries; by the early twentieth century the fish stocks were less bountiful.*

DRINK IN SUSSEX

'Stand fast root, fear well top
Pray God to send us a howling good crop'

TRADITIONAL APPLE WASSAILING SONG

Sussex is strong in the production of DRINK (wine, beer, cider and all their non-alcoholic siblings), and is growing more so as the fashion for micro – in BREWERIES and everything else – continues to hold. People who enjoy the pleasures of Brighton now may be less aware of its brief but fashionable background as a spa, where sea water was drunk as a cure for all sorts of maladies. Looking out from Brighton beach today, most will decide to stick with the other refreshments on offer.

A Sussex drinking song

On Sussex Downs, where I was bred,
In rains where autumn lanes are red,
Where Aran tumbles in his bed
And dusty gales go by.

Where branches, bare on vert and glen
And merry hills are whitening then;
I drink strong ale with gentle-men,
Which no one can deny, deny,
Which no one can deny, deny.

In cold November off I go,
And turn my face against the snow;
And watch the wind where ere it blow,
Because my heart is high.

'Till I settle me down in Steyning to sing
Of the girls I've met in my wandering;
And all I mean to do in Spring
Which no one can deny, deny,
Which no one can deny, deny.

'Tho times be hard and fortunes tough,
The ways be foul and the weather rough;
We are of stout south country stock
Who cannot have strong ale enough

From Crowborough Top to Ditchling Down,
From Hurstpierpoint to Arundel town,
The girls are fine, the ale is brown;
Which no one can deny, deny,
Which no one can deny, deny.

© HILAIRE BELLOC, 1870-1953

Nowadays more usually associated with his *Cautionary Tales* – doggerel rhymes in which poorly behaved children meet with appropriate ends – BELLOC was actually one of the most prolific writers of the early twentieth century, covering a variety of genres. Asked why he wrote so much, he said that it was because his children were 'howling for pearls and caviar'. This Sussex drinking song is an oddity; it is still sung on the folk circuit.

Taking the waters

Early in Brighton's history, when it was still the fishing village of BRIGHTHELMSTONE, its first transformation was as a health centre where the fashionable came to bathe and drink sea water. In 1750 RICHARD RUSSELL, a Lewes man and a doctor, published his treatise, *A Dissertation concerning the use of Sea-Water in the Diseases of the Glands*, which made astonishing claims for that very basic commodity. He believed that drinking and bathing in sea water could cure consumption, digestive problems and toothache, and relieve many other symptoms besides. The core of Russell's ascetic regime was a strict diet and controlled exercise, so the sea water may have been incidental. Whatever the truth of it, by 1754, he had moved to Brighthelmstone and set up a large establishment there, where he entertained more than 400 patients a year. He died in 1759.

Six Sussex vineyards

We know that the Romans grew vines in Britain, and over the last twenty years, British WINE has again begun to gain a reasonable reputation. Here are six SUSSEX VINEYARDS (a random selection from a broad choice), each producing its own distinctive wine.

1. ***Breaky Bottom***, *Northease Farm, between Lewes and Rodmell*
   Started in the mid-1970s, with some award-winning wines. Principally growing the Seyval Blanc variety.
2. ***Nyetimber Vineyard***, *West Chiltington*
   Best-known for sparkling wines, with a growing reputation internationally.
3. ***Rotherfield Vineyard***, *Rotherham*
   A new contender, all-organic, with just four acres (nearly two hectares) of vines.
4. ***Lurgashall Winery***, *near Petworth*
   Wines from fruit, vegetables and herbs. Some unusual and exotic flavours.
5. ***Nutbourne Vineyards***, *near Pulborough*
   One of the most varied vineyards in Sussex, growing seven types of grape.
6. ***Bolney Wine Estate***, *near Haywards Heath*

☛ *Growing from 3 to 22 acres (1 to 9 hectares) in its 30-plus-year history, this last estate has one of the widest ranges of distribution of the county's vineyards.*

SUSSEX INNS

'Blann's it is the beer for me, A pint of it's so handy,
It's as fine as any wine, and strong as any brandy.'

DRINKING SONG CREDITED TO **MICHAEL BLANN**, SHOREHAM, 1880S

As a widely travelled county with a number of ports and busy coastal traffic, Sussex has its fair share of historic INNS and PUBS. REAL ALE ENTHUSIASTS will find plenty in the area to interest them, but the buildings themselves, and their histories, are often engaging in their own right. Many date from the sixteenth century, or earlier; most can offer a ghost or two, or some smugglers' tales, to embroider a drink in the bar.

Oddly named pubs

Strange names for PUBS are not limited to Sussex – but it can offer a handful of real oddities.

The *Dog & Bacon* at Horsham is one; the *White Horse* at Chilgrove is ostensibly straightforward enough – except that, for twenty years, its sign showed a tabby cat rather than the horse one would expect. Local lore held that the signpainter could execute a respectable cat, but couldn't render the legs of a horse at all. There's a pub in Yapton called the *Shoulder of Mutton & Cucumbers*, although whether these ingredients commonly made a dinner in past times is unknown.

Perhaps the oddest is the *Guinea Pig* in East Grinstead. Guinea pigs are not indigenous to Sussex – instead, the name is in tribute to the GUINEA PIG CLUB, a group of pilots injured in the BATTLE OF BRITAIN. Some horribly disfigured by fire, they were sent to the burns unit at East Grinstead Hospital, run by SIR ARCHIBALD MCINDOE. The name of the club – only men in the unit, or who had been in the unit, could join – reflected the experimental nature of the job Sir Archibald was doing; plastic surgery was still at so early a stage that he was – inevitably – experimental in his techniques.

The pub sign shows a guinea pig with the wings of the RAF insignia, seated above a burning plane. The hospital is nearby.

An elaborate haunting

So many pubs and inns in Sussex have a ghost that it takes an exceptional tale to stand out. The fourteenth-century *Mermaid Inn* in Rye has what must be one of the most well-organised ghostly scenarios anywhere, played out at irregular intervals to an admiring audience. A pair of duellists of unknown date and origin fight their way through the public rooms. One is eventually killed, and the victor drags the ghostly 'corpse' through the inn and drops the body through a trapdoor. According to hearsay (although those who relate the story were always there!) the pair have enacted their drama for more than one research study over the last century.

FACTBOX

If you want to drink where the Prince Regent drank, THE KING'S ARMS, *at 56, George Street, Brighton, was a royal favourite and is still serving.*

Smallest pub? Oldest pub?

The *Hole In The Wall* in Brighton lays claim to being England's smallest pub; 'smallest pub in the south' is the rather vague title claimed by *The Blue Anchor* at Barcombe. Neither holds the record in any official source – but they are certainly very snug sites for a drink. Sussex is probably on safer ground claiming at least some of the oldest inns in the country: the *Mermaid* in Rye dates from 1420, and the *Swan Inn* at Fittleworth has records stretching back to 1382, but the *Star Inn* at Alfriston pips them both with proven thirteenth-century origins.

The practice of wife-selling

WIFE-SELLING was not infrequent in nineteenth-century Sussex. Some cases of which there is reliable evidence include:

BRIGHTON, 1799, Mr Staines sold his wife to Mr Marten for 5s and 8 pots of beer.

NINFIELD, 1790, at the village inn, an unnamed man sold his wife for half a pint of gin (but bought her back the next day).

HORSHAM, 1825, a journeyman blacksmith sold his wife for £2 5*s*.

YAPTON, 1898, at the *Shoulder of Mutton and Cucumbers*, Mr Marley sold his wife to Mr White for 7s 6d and a quart of beer.

☛ *The village inn was frequently the scene of these bargains, and most are distinguished by a quantity of drink consumed.*

FARMING IN SUSSEX

'The original red Sussex ox was always a kindly and handsome beast, and a good worker.'

W.H. HUDSON, *NATURE IN DOWNLAND*, 1923

Offering excellent land both for pasture and for farming (the rich coastal plain lends itself to arable, and the high Downs to grazing), Sussex has been an AGRICULTURAL COUNTY since records began. Even since many of the farms amalgamated over the last century, creating larger areas, but often less individual in character, smallholding continued to thrive in Sussex, and is still popular today, probably in part as a result of the number of country-sick incomers from London that the county attracts.

Saxon farmers

One of the first documents of individual rights, the *Rectitudines Singularum Personarum*, drawn up in the eleventh century, gives us a good idea of what a typical smallholding farmer might own. THE SUSSEX FREEMAN (gebur, from which the unlovely word 'boor' derives) would have usually been answerable to his churl, who in turn would have answered to the local thane, or larger landholder.

A gebur paid ten pennies to his lord on every MICHELMAS DAY, plus tithes to the church.

In return, he received:

- *Seven acres of land.*
- *Two oxen to plough it.*
- *Six sheep.*
- *Tools to work with.*

Sussex hens

One of the success stories of Sussex breeding, has been in its POULTRY; equally good for meat and eggs, and popular with smallholders everywhere, the Sussex chicken is medium-to-large (averaging 9lb for a cock and 7lb for a hen), elegant to look at, good tempered and easy to keep. Quite a strong recommendation to those who just want a few hens in the garden. The paler colours are allegedly the better layers.

The seven colour varieties are:

Red – Rich red with black points in the cocks, slightly paler in the hens.

Brown – Deep brown with black points in the cocks; paler hens.

Light – A white body with elegant black and white striping to the neck and black wing- and tail-tips.

Buff – Similar striping to the Light, with the main body a gingery buff.

Silver – A black body with silver-laced feathers throughout.

White – Pure white hens and cocks.

Speckled – A smart mix of deep brown and black feathers, each with a white tip, giving the bird its characteristic 'freckled' appearance.

Honey as business

BEEKEEPING is a longtime interest in Sussex, and it has a thriving bee-keepers' association. For anyone who just thought HONEY was honey, here's a list of the local classes in the national honey show, in which Sussex keepers make regular and distinguished appearances:

- *Two jars light* . . . .
- *Two jars medium* . . . .
- *Two jars dark* . . . .
- *Two jars softset* . . . .
- *Two jars ling heather* . . . .
- *One section free from ling heather* . .
- *One section ling heather* . . . .
- *One comb, any source, any size, suitable for extraction* . . . .
- *Two containers of cut comb, free from ling heather* . . . .
- *Two jars ling heather blend extracted, naturally crystallised (not stirred)* . . . .
- *Beeswax, one piece, weight between 7 and 9oz (200-255g), not less than 3/4in (19mm) thick* . . . .
- *Mead, dry (one bottle)*. . . . .
- *Mead, sweet (one bottle)* . . . .

For the curious non-beekeeper, LING HEATHER is one of the most popular honey flavours, but produces a very thick mixture which will not pour, and which is thus difficult to extract – hence the stress on single 'sections' of Ling Heather.

Prodigious cattle

DANIEL DEFOE was particularly impressed by the sheer size of the Sussex cattle:

> *'Near Stenning (sic), the famous Sir John Fagg had a noble antient seat... being entertained at his house, in the year 1697, he show'd me in his park four bullocks of his own breeding, and of his own feeding, of so prodigious a size, and so excessively overgrown by fat, that I never saw any thing like them... some London butchers came down to see them, and in my hearing offered Sir John six and twenty pound a head for them, but he refused it; and when I mov'd him afterward to take the money, he said No, he was resolv'd to have them to Smithfield himself, that he might say he had the four biggest bullocks in England at market...By this may be judg'd something of the largeness of the cattle in the Wild of Kent and Sussex, for it is all the same, of which I mention'd something before, and for this reason I tell the story.'*

☛ *Defoe's detailed observation is impressive for someone who was not himself a farmer.*

COUNTY SOCIETY

'Society is composed of two classes: those with more dinners than appetite, and those with more appetite than dinners.'

NICOLAS DE CHAMFORT

SOCIETY in Sussex has always been various. Not only is the county home to some of the oldest families in Britain, but it is also famous for producing a trenchant breed of yeomen and women. 'We wun't be druv' – loosely translatable as 'You can't push us around, so don't try' – has long been Sussex's unofficial motto, and a suitable one for the county that produced THOMAS PAINE, and has always had a keen awareness of its own rights.

Not quite like other counties

STELLA GIBBONS' comic masterpiece *Cold Comfort Farm*, published in 1932, may be the most famous novel set in Sussex. Its heroine, FLORA POSTE, with a modern outlook and a can-do attitude, sets out – to the aghast amusement of her friends – to organise her glum cousins the Starkadders, who live in deep rural squalor in the village of HOWLING.

'"Sussex...", mused Mrs Smiling. "I don't much like the sound of that. Do they live on a decaying farm?"
"I am afraid they do", confessed Flora... She reminded herself that Sussex, when all was said and done, was not quite like other counties...
"Well", said Mrs Smiling, "it sounds an appalling place..."'

But *Cold Comfort Farm* is actually itself a parody of those writers who, steeped in D.H. Lawrence, produced great quantities of melodramatically 'authentic' novels between the 1910s and the early '30s. MARY WEBBE and SHEILA KAYE-SMITH were two of the foremost stars of this rather grim genre, in particular Kaye-Smith, known as 'the Sussex novelist' as she set the vast majority of her books in East Sussex. Ironically, the book that first brought Kaye-Smith fame, the gloomy and successful *Sussex Gorse*, published in 1916, is almost forgotten today.

Centres of rural life

Sussex is full of places offering effective insights into the past. It's awash with museums and centres where old crafts, from smithing to basket-weaving, are demonstrated, which give the onlooker the strong sensation that time really can be brushed aside.

Five of the best:

1. *The Weald & Downland Open Air Museum, Singleton,* *near Chichester*
Buildings – largely medieval and Tudor – brought from all over the country and re-erected. Ancient breeds of farm animals live on site.

2. *Ripley's Museum of Rural Life,* *Robertsbridge*
Complete period shop interiors, a village garage, and demonstrations of smithing.

3. *Fishbourne Roman Palace*
A surprisingly vivid evocation of everyday life in Roman Sussex, with an effective video presentation.

4. *Michelham Priory*
With a working water mill, complete with demonstrations of grinding flour.

5. *Amberley Working Museum,* *Arundel*
Covering 36 acres, with vintage buses, a working locomotive, and many resident practitioners of life crafts, demonstrating as broom- and pipe-making, foundry and smithing skills. Plus a printing press and workshop.

A Sussex huntsman

Lines from a gravestone at CHARLTON which seem to capture the mood of eighteenth-century hunting society perfectly – classless, yet with an eye to a lord; reverent, yet loving a laugh:

Near this place lies interred
THOMAS JOHNSON
who departed this life at Charlton
December 20th, 1744.
From his early inclination to foxhounds
he soon became
an experienced hunstman. His knowledge
in the profession,
wherein he had no superior, and hardly
an equal, joined to his honesty in
every other particular, recommended him
to the service, and gain'd him the
approbation of several of the nobility and
gentry (A long list of lords, too long to
quote here, follows)...
the last master whom he served, and in
whose service he died, was Charles, Duke
of Richmond Lennox and Aubigny,
who erected this monument to the
memory of a good and faithful servant as
a reward to the deceased and an
incitement to the living.
Go thou and do likewise.

ST LUKE, CHAP X. VER. XXXVII

Here Johnson lies. What Hunter can deny
Old honest TOM the tribute of a sigh?
Deaf is the Ear, which caught the
opening sound,
Dumb is that Tongue, which cheered
the Hills around.
Unpleasing Truth, Death hunts us
from our Birth,
In view, and Men, like Foxes,
take to Earth.

PETS & COMPANIONS

'Animals are such agreeable friends – they ask no questions, they pass no criticisms.'

GEORGE ELIOT, *SCENES OF CLERICAL LIFE*, 1857

Traditional farmers and squires of Sussex had their HUNTERS and their DOGS as companions. But Sussex has also boasted a wide range of creatives and eccentrics, and their choice of PETS was not always so conservative. Rather sinisterly, WALTER POTTER, the renowned taxidermist, referred to the animals he used with such a liberal hand in his masterworks, as his 'pets', though none was actually alive.

The Bloomsbury marmoset

THE BLOOMSBURY GROUP were fond of animals, and cats and dogs in their Sussex households at CHARLESTON and RODMELL were commonplace. A more unusual pet, kept by Leonard, was Mitz the marmoset (a type of tiny monkey) given to him by Victor Rothschild. Opinions were divided on Mitz, who travelled everywhere with the Woolfs, toured Nazi Germany, and sat at meals at Monks House, feeding off scraps. Lady Ottoline Morell admired her; most of the Bells, on the other hand, loathed her – Vanessa calling her 'that horrid little monkey' and Quentin Bell, Virginia's nephew, went much further, accusing the marmoset of having a vicious temper and a face 'like Doctor Goebbels' . An acclaimed novel about Mitz's life, *Mitz, the Marmoset of Bloomsbury*, by Sigrid Nunez, was published in 1996.

'A FAIR DOG FOR HUNTING'

The only dog named for the county, the Sussex spaniel is a heavy-set retriever with a curling coat of a rich liver colour. It is best suited to field sports, well tempered, and quite noisy. Its popularity has spread to the US, where it is known as a good, if 'barky', retrieving dog, with a soft mouth. It is still a comparatively rare breed.

Skydiving dogs

With its precipitous cliffs, the Sussex coastline is not the safest walking country for over-excited dogs. The Sussex record for a fall by a living dog is held by Henry, a retriever, who fell over 140ft from the cliffs near BEACHY HEAD (Sussex's famous suicide plunge spot), landed in the sea, and swam to safety with a few bruises and a broken leg. Henry isn't the furthest faller in England, though. That record is held by a terrier in Dorset who fell over 300ft and survived to tell the tale with just a few bruises and a cut lip.

The Ringmer tortoise

Those who pass through Ringmer may be puzzled by the central appearance of a TORTOISE on the village sign. But Timothy Tortoise is famous in the area; in 1740, he (or more probably a she) was bought from a sailor at Chichester for half a crown and came to live with MRS REBECCA SNOOKE at Delves House in Ringmer. Mrs Snooke's nephew was the naturalist GILBERT WHITE. He enjoyed making a study of Timothy on his annual visits to Ringmer and conducted a number of experiments using him. On Mrs Snooke's death in 1780, he took the tortoise to live with him at Selborne, and notes and observations on the 'old Sussex tortoise' can be read in his great work, *The Natural History and Antiquities of Selborne* (1789). Timothy's shell lives on after him (or her) at the Natural History Museum in London.

Bramber Museum

The 'companions' of the amateur taxidermist, WALTER POTTER, at his small museum in BRAMBER, were so extraordinary that the local railway station had to extend its platform to accommodate the sheer numbers of the visitors who came to see them. Potter was self-taught, and his tableaux placed extraordinary numbers of animals in 'human' situations. *The Original Death of Cock Robin* contains every one of the birds named in the rhyme, omitting only the kite (uncommon then as now in Sussex).

Potter spent all his time acquiring and stuffing animals for new, ever-more-elaborate scenes and referred to them as his friends. He died in 1918, and in the 1970s the contents of his museum were sold and moved, first to Arundel, then to Jamaica Inn, in Cornwall, and finally auctioned and dispersed in 2003.

Eight tableaux that could be seen at Bramber (later Potter's) Museum

1. *The Kittens' Wedding* . . . .
2. *The Original Death and Burial of Cock Robin* . . . .
3. *A Friend in Need* (A rat assisting another from a trap) . . . .
4. *The Death* (Duelling squirrels) . . .
5. *The Rabbits' Schoolroom* . . . .
6. *The Kittens' Tea Party* . . . .
7. *The House that Jack Built* (Complete with stuffed kitten, puppy, and miniaturised cow) . . . .
8. *The Squirrels' Club* . . . .

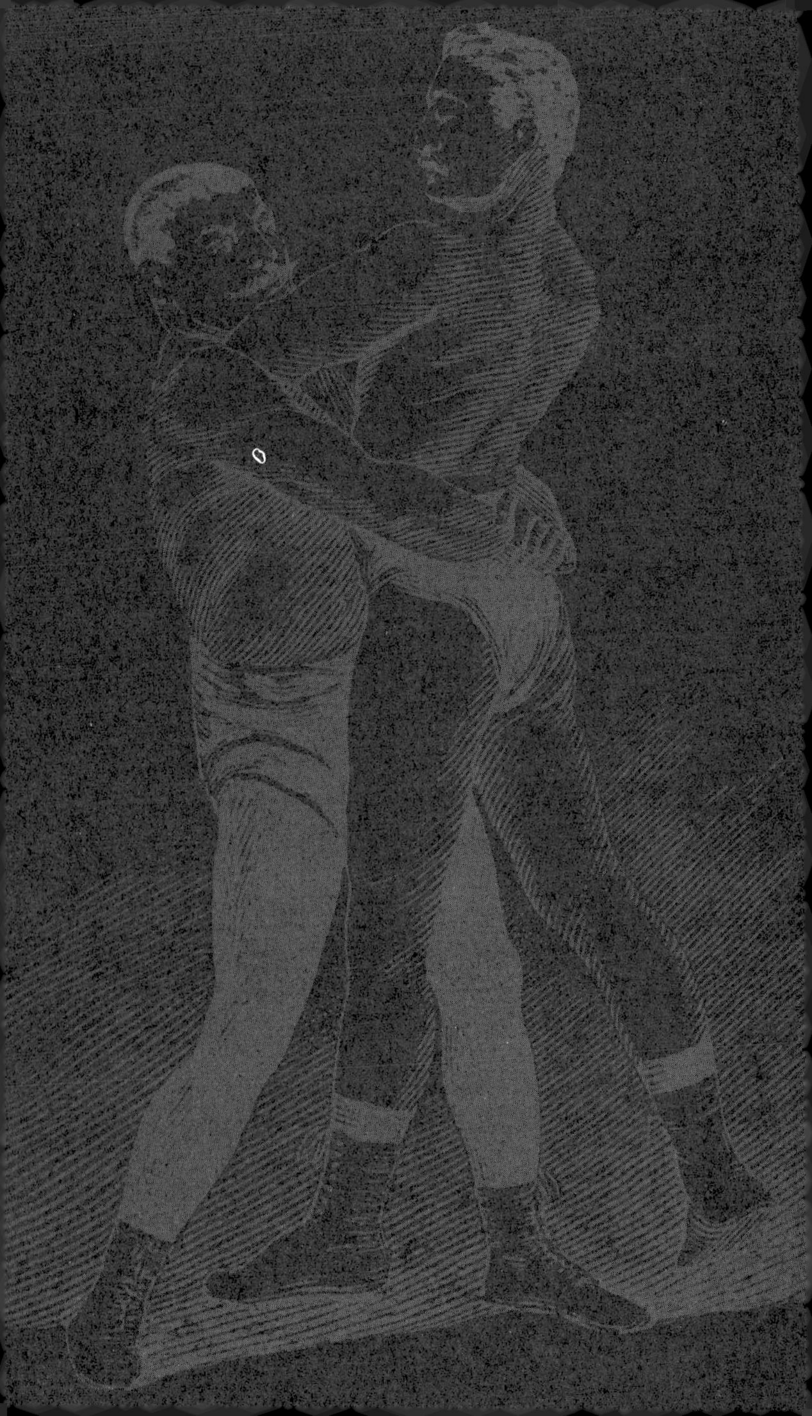

CHAPTER FIVE

SUSSEX PASTIMES

The crafts, skills and games of Sussex are as individual as the county's other aspects. You may never have heard of toad (the game) or stoolball, but both are popular and played competitively. As is marbles, although the particular draw there is that Sussex hosts the world's marble championships, despite rival competitions setting up in perhaps less surprising places, like Prague. At the more highbrow end of the scale, Sussex has always thrown out a powerful lure to more intellectual incomers, too. Bloomsbury used it as its out-of-town base (although Virginia Woolf, 'dressed like a vagrant' never felt particularly at home with the locals), and it has had more than its fair share of rich patrons and creative writers and artists.

Patron saint of Sussex authors must be Rudyard Kipling, who inevitably crops up over and over again in any account of artistic life. He lived here for 40 years, and put down deep roots in Sussex; his anthem to the county's charms is reprinted hundreds of times a year – and, although unfashionable, remains the most sincere tribute ever written to a landscape. And, like other visiting grandees, Sussex made space for him and, once he had retreated from a roadside house in Rottingdean to a more secluded home, let him be. If the county's natives were independent (the more admirable companion to obstinacy) then, too, they admired independence in others, and have tolerated each to his own pastime for centuries, just leaving them be to get on with whatever pleases them.

POETS & WRITERS

'I am very fond of fresh air and royalties.'

DAISY ASHFORD

Sussex has given birth to and hosted a full complement of both poets and writers. SHELLEY was born in Sussex, but left it as soon as possible; others as diverse as VIRGINIA and LEONARD WOOLF, HENRY JAMES and RUDYARD KIPLING lived there for significant periods of their creative lives. Remote in atmosphere although not, after the mid-nineteenth century and the coming of the railway, in fact, it met the needs of many writers to be near to London and to 'life', yet to have sufficient seclusion in which to work in peace.

The prophet of food

The grave of the food writer ELIZABETH DAVID, born Gwynne, can be seen in the churchyard of St Peter's at FOLKINGTON, near Wilmington. Her father, Rupert Gwynne, was MP for Eastbourne and she grew up in some style at Wootten Manor nearby. Although she spent none of her adult life in Sussex, her roots remained there, and her elaborate stone reflects the huge influence that her elegant writing had on attitudes to food in England. Recalling the covers of her first books, with illustrations by the artist John Minton, it is topped by the carved relief of a cooking pot surrounded by the highly flavoured and scarce ingredients that she brought alive in the 1950s for a war-worn Britain: garlic, lemons, aubergines, peppers and artichokes.

A hymn to Sussex

Few writers are as unabashed about declaring their allegiance to a place as RUDYARD KIPLING was about Sussex. His poem, *Sussex*, written in 1900, might not be considered among his best – to the contemporary reader some of its 11 verses may seem rather saccharine, but there can be absolutely no doubt of their sincerity:

'God gives all men all earth to love,
But since man's heart is small
Ordains for each one spot shall prove
Beloved over all.
Each to his choice, and I rejoice
The lot has fallen to me
In a fair ground – in a fair ground -
Yea, Sussex by the sea!'

Kipling lived in Sussex from 1897 until his death in 1935, first at Rottingdean, then, when his fame grew too great and the intrusions into his privacy too disturbing, in the beautiful seventeenth-century house BATEMANS, near Burwash. The latter is owned by the National Trust and is open to the public.

Quotes from The Young Visiters

DAISY ASHFORD's childhood masterpiece is often quoted, but her turn of phrase is neat enough to stand up to repetition. It's much better than her spelling or her punctuation.

1. *'My life will be sour grapes and ashes without you.'*
2. *'I certainly love you madly you are to me like a Heathen god...'*
3. *'I am not quite a gentleman, but you would hardly notice it.'*
4. *His bathroom had '...a tip-up bason and a hose thing for washing your head'*
5. *'My own idear is that these things are as piffle before the wind.'*

The Young Visiters [sic] was written when Ashford was nine and living in Lewes, to amuse her mother who was ill at the time, making her Sussex's youngest published novelist. Her only other full-length work, *The Hangman's Daughter*, was allegedly completed by the time she was 13, and that was an end to her writing; burnt out, she married a market gardener in Norfolk and never finished another work.

Field and Hedgerow

RICHARD JEFFERIES, one of the great nature writers, died at Goring in 1887, aged only 39, and is buried in BROADWATER CEMETARY in Worthing. His gravestone has the inscription, 'Prose poet of England's fields and woodlands'. He captures the atmosphere of an early Sussex morning in a way few writers could manage.

'Dark specks beneath the white summer clouds, the swifts, the black albatross of our skis, moved on their unwearied wings ... The corn was tall and green, the hops looked well, the foxglove was stirring, the delicious atmosphere of summer, sun-laden and scented, filled the deep valleys; a morning of the richest beauty and deepest repose ... Nature is absolutely still every day of the week, and proceeds with the utmost indifference to days and dates.'

☛ *Field and Hedgerow, being the last Essays of Richard Jefferies, published posthumously in 1889.*

PAINTERS & SCULPTORS

'Art is the tree of life'

WILLIAM BLAKE

Sussex has been home to plenty of ARTISTIC ACTIVITY during its history, and it has long been a refuge for creative souls searching after peace and quiet or a rural 'authenticity' depending on their bent. Not every incomer 'takes' – BLAKE, for example, after a difficult end to an otherwise happy sojourn to Felpham, concluded that he could see visions only in London – but the county has offered both inspiring landscape and, often, generous patrons.

A much-travelled kiss

In 1904, a version of AUGUSTE RODIN's famous KISS, was bought by the rich American art collector Edward Perry Warren, who lived in LEWES HOUSE on School Hill in Lewes in the early twentieth century. Seeing and admiring the first marble version of the sculpture, which had been commissioned by the French government, Warren commissioned Rodin to make another, specifying that the male genitals be fully shown, rather than genteelly draped. Whether it was the fact that the requested detailing was still extremely sketchy or that the work disappointed in some other way, Warren stored it in his stables after it arrived in 1904, then made a permanent loan of it to Lewes Council, who placed it in the town hall in 1913. The story then takes on the aspect of farce – the sculpture was far, far too lewd for local sensibilities, and a movement was got up to ban it, led by Miss Fowler-Tutt, a redoubtable local headmistress. First it was draped, then hidden behind screens, and finally returned to Warren, in whose outhouses it languished until his death in 1928. Eventually it was loaned to the Tate Gallery but returned for a fleeting visit to Lewes, where it was welcomed more warmly second time around, in 1999.

Death of a muse

One of the odder – and sadder – stories around the rackety private lives of the Impressionists concerns LIZZIE SIDDAL, muse to MILLAIS, HOLMAN HUNT and ROSSETTI, among others, and long-term lover of Rossetti. Lizzie was the inspiration for Millais' *Ophelia* and (posthumously) for Rossetti's *Beatrice* – it was while posing in an inadequately heated bath for *Ophelia* that she caught the cold which seemed to be the precursor of the constant ill-health that troubled her from 1852 onwards. In 1862, depressed by her illness and the uneven state of her relationship with Rossetti, she took an overdose of laudanum at the CHATHAM PLACE house she shared with him in Hastings. Overcome by grief, Rossetti placed a notebook containing the only transcriptions of a number of his poems in Lizzie's coffin before she was buried in Highgate Cemetery, but he regretted it later on and, bizarrely, he obtained permission for her body to be exhumed so that he could reclaim them from the coffin (subsequent readers noted that the notebook was somewhat wormeaten, but that most of the poems were still legible). Lizzie's continuing battles with illness and depression had lasted for fully ten years; not long before her death, Rossetti had written to Ford Madox Ford,

> *'she has seemed ready to die daily, and more than once a day...'.*

A stone carved with Rossetti's and Lizzie's initials allegedly still exists on OLD ROAR ROAD in Hastings, near the waterfall which, then far more secluded and romantically hung about with ferns, was a favourite walk for lovers in Victorian times.

Landscape and art

CHRIS DRURY, one of the foremost land artists working in Britain today, creates works that are integral to the spaces around them. He has worked all over the world from Japan to Antarctica and America, but has often created site-specific pieces for Sussex, around landscapes and sites that are familiar to him (he lives in Lewes).

Five Sussex works

1992 *Cuckoo Dome*, woodlands, Sussex
1994 . . . . *Vortex*, Lewes
1999 . . . . . . *Holding Light*, Brighton
2001 . . . . *Rhythms of the Heart*, Conquest Hospital, Hastings
2004 . . . . *Heart of Reeds*, Lewes

Of these, the last is the largest, and promises to have a long life as both landscape and work of art. It is formed of a created reed bed that is arranged to demonstrate the patterns of blood flow to the heart. In summer, the rich growth of the reeds almost obscures the heartlines, but it can be seen from a specially constructed viewing mound and from various viewpoints on the Downs above Lewes all year round.

BEACHLIFE

'Bugger Bognor!'

APOCRYPHAL DYING WORDS OF **GEORGE V**

'DR BRIGHTON', RICHARD RUSSELL, of Lewes, was one of the first to advocate the healthy properties of sea bathing (and, indeed, sea drinking) in the 1730s, but a host of others swiftly followed him, and villages previously peopled by fishermen and farmers found themselves in the middle of a building boom. Brighton was pre-eminent by the early nineteenth century, made fashionable by the royal connection, but Eastbourne, Hastings, Worthing and Bognor all enjoyed massive growth, and the modern notion of the seaside as a place for rest and relaxation was born.

Piers

At the beginning of the twentieth century Britain still had around a hundred SEASIDE PIERS, and they were widely used for everything from fishing and promenading to concerts and fair rides.

Today that total has shrunk to 54, of which Sussex accounts for six. Of those, three are still open to the public.

EUGENIUS BIRCH was king of English pier builders – this Victorian engineer had a lightness and elegance of touch which can still be seen in those examples of his work that haven't been overloaded with subsequent amendments and additions – EASTBOURNE PIER remains the least messed-around, and a pleasure to visit. The technical challenges of piers posed few problems to a man who had overseen the construction of the railway between Delhi and Calcutta.

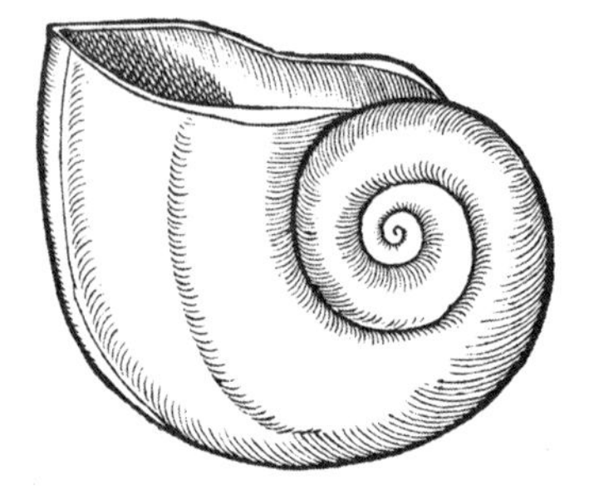

Pier	*Construction dates*	*Architect*	*Original length*	*Condition*
BOGNOR REGIS	1863-65	*Bognor Promenade Company*	Not known	*Derelict*
BRIGHTON				
PALACE PIER	1891-9	*R. St George Moore*	533.3m	*Open to the public*
WEST PIER	1863-6	*Eugenius Birch*	337.8m	*Collapsed; a fragmentary skeleton*
EASTBOURNE	1866-70	*Eugenius Birch*	303m	*Open to the public*
HASTINGS	1869-72	*Eugenius Birch*	275m	*Closed*
WORTHING	1861-2	*Sir Robert Rawlinson*	291m	*Open to the public*

A lost Austen seaside

JANE AUSTEN's novel *Sanditon* was left incomplete on her death in 1817. A pity for the seaside literature of Sussex, as well as for Austen-philes. Situated at an imaginary spot between Eastbourne and Hastings, Sanditon takes on different identities for the reader according to which character is speaking:

'...Sanditon itself – everybody has heard of Sanditon [cries the enthusiastic Mr Parker] – the favourite for a young and rising bathing-place, certainly the favourite spot of all that are to be found along the coast of Sussex – the most favoured by Nature, and promising to be the most chosen by Man.'

'Yes, I have heard of Sanditon,' replied Mr H. 'Every five years, one hears of some new place or other starting up by the sea, and growing the fashion. How they can half of them be filled is the wonder! Where people can be found with money or time to go to them!'

THE HASTINGS NET SHOPS

At the working end of Hastings' long stretch of beach, the Stade, stands a handful of buildings unique in the British Isles. Two or even three storeys high, they look like bathing huts that have suffered a growth spurt. They're the fishing fleet's 'net shops', in which the nets are hung to dry, and they're still used today.

SUSSEX FOLLIES

'One would think that St. Paul's Cathedral had come to Brighton and pupped.'

SIDNEY SMITH, OF BRIGHTON PAVILION

Sussex can boast many FOLLIES, although it is not always certain that their creators intended them as such – some were built as memorials or markers to a specific event, whether within a noble family or of more general importance. And although the golden age of the folly was the eighteenth century, and literally dozens of examples dot the curves of the South Downs, a striking new example will occasionally join them – a brick folly in the shape of a camel has recently been built at Milland, near Chichester.

The follies of Mad Jack

One of the most colourful characters in early nineteenth-century Sussex was MAD JACK FULLER. MP for East Sussex, bon viveur, and a well-known and respected patron of the arts, he was also a builder of numerous follies around his estate at BRIGHTLING PARK. Probably the most famous of them is the SUGARLOAF, so called because its conical shape resembles that of the solid loaves of sugar, wrapped in blue paper, that were usual before lump or powdered sugar were invented. The myth of the Sugarloaf is that it was built in a single night to meet a bet Fuller made with a neighbour that he could see the spire of Dallington Church from his house. When he returned home, he realised that he would have to build a fake spire to win the bet – hence the Sugarloaf's conical, spire-like shape, and its location, a mile from his house. Fitted out as a feasible, though inconvenient, house inside, with two floors linked by a ladder, the Sugarloaf was occupied until the 1930s, although it's not known by whom.

Seven Sussex towers

The tower is by far the most common form a folly takes – wonderful views as well as a chance for seclusion might be considered one of its perks. Here are seven of the most interesting. Some are intact, others near-ruins.

- GIBRALTER TOWER, 1792
  near Heathfield
- PITSHILL TOWER
  Tillington, near Petworth
- RACTON TOWER, 1772
  Uppark Estate, Aldsworth
- SAXONBURY TOWER
  Eridge Estate, near Heathfield
- TOAT MONUMENT, 1827
- UPPERTON MONUMENT, 1800
  Grounds of Petworth House, Petworth
- VANDALIAN TOWER, 1774

The Pepperpot Palace

Whether you think BRIGHTON PAVILION should be considered as a palace or a folly depends on your viewpoint – today it has the charm of the eccentric and the unexpected. In the early nineteenth century, the period during which the PRINCE REGENT was gradually transforming a previously workmanlike and none-too-fancy farmhouse into an oriental fantasy, rampant criticism left little doubt as to public opinion.

'How can one describe such a piece of architecture? The style is a mixture of Moorish, Tartar, Gothic, and Chinese and all in stone and iron. It is a whim which has already cost £700,000, and it is still not fit to live in...'

PRINCESS LIEVEN
LETTER TO METTERNICH, 27 OCTOBER, 1820

'The queerest of all the queer sights I've set sight on
Is, the whatd'ye-call-'t thing, here, THE FOLLY at Brighton
The outside – huge teapots, all drill'd round with holes,
Relieved by extinguishers, sticking on poles:
The inside – all tea-things, and dragons, and bells,
The show rooms – all show, the sleeping rooms – cells...'

WILLIAM HONE
EXTRACT FROM VERSES

A rather sugary poem of support carries much less weight than the acidly expressed opprobrium:

'Around the beauteous lawn, gay buildings rise,
There the Pavilion woos admiring eyes...
And as each scene admiring we explore,
It seems enchantment all, some magic bower...'

MARY LLOYD
BRIGHTON: A POEM, 1809

FIREWORKS IN LEWES

'Throughout recorded history, it has taken very little persuasion to get English people to make a bonfire.'

THE OXFORD DICTIONARY OF ENGLISH FOLKLORE

Any description of fireworks in Sussex must focus on LEWES, the county town of East Sussex. While plenty of GUY FAWKES celebrations take place in other parts of the county, Lewes is justly famous for its bonfire societies and the huge celebrations held on each BONFIRE NIGHT, drawing an estimated 20,000 visitors to the small town every 5 November. Bonfire Night is celebrated all over Britain – but why is it such a focus in this particular site?

BONFIRE SOCIETIES	FOUNDED	MOTTO	'SMUGGLERS' LIVERY
Cliffe Bonfire Society	1853	*Nulli Secundus*	Black-and-white striped jersey and cap
Commercial Square	1855	*For Independence*	Black-and-gold striped jersey and red cap
Lewes Borough Society	1853	*Death or Glory*	Blue-and-white striped jersey and red cap
Southover 2005	re-formed	*Advance*	Red-and-black striped jersey and red cap
South Street	1913	*Faithful unto death*	Brown-and-white striped jersey and red cap
Waterloo	re-formed 1964	*True to Each*	Red-and-white striped jersey and cap
Nevill Juvenile	1968	*We Dare*	Green-and-white striped jersey, green cap

FACTBOX

The 'smugglers' caps and jerseys worn by the foot soldiers of each society were, with blacked faces, originally intended to disguise the Bonfire Boys in case they were caught out in any misdeed.

The six adult societies always celebrate on 5 November (or the day before if it falls on a Sunday). Nevill Juvenile have their own junior firework display which is slightly – but only slightly – tamer than the adult version, on a different night.

Why Lewes?

Lewes had a vested interest in the defeat of any Catholic plot because of the town's bitter memory of the LEWES MARTYRS – 17 Protestants who were burned at the stake there between 1555 and 1557, during the reign of Mary Tudor. When the day of 5 November was declared a public holiday after the 1605 CATESBY plot to blow up Parliament was discovered (Guy Fawkes was a minor player in the affair, but was caught red-handed in the building, and so gave his name to subsequent legend), firework displays became fixed as a way of celebrating it. By the end of the eighteenth century Lewes was already overrun with gangs of youths, known as the BONFIRE BOYS, who, every year, drank, caroused and generally caused mayhem through the town. The first societies were intended to bring some order to BONFIRE NIGHT, and, in giving the different gangs a structure, it worked. Today, each society traditionally takes a different route to process through Lewes, wearing elaborate fancy dress, and bearing vast effigies – often of GUY FAWKES and the Pope, but also including any other contemporary and unpopular figure, and finishes at its own bonfire site where an immense pyre is waiting to burn them. Today, the celebrations are energetic, wild, and very, very noisy, but they are not as dangerous as in former times.

Traditional rhyme

A penny loaf to feed the Pope
A farthing o'cheese to choke him
A pint of beer to rinse it down
A faggot of sticks to burn him.
Burn him in a tub of tar
Burn him like a blazing star
Burn his body from his head
Then we'll say ol' Pope is dead.
Hip hip hoorah!
Hip hip hoorah hoorah!

This verse is rarely included in bonfire ceremonies today on account of its anti-Catholic sentiments, but it is mentioned in sources stretching back to the early eighteenth century.

The processions

Every society's PROCESSION involves a large number of its foot soldiers (who all wear the society's uniform of caps and striped jerseys), plus a 'bishop' who is invested for the evening, and sometimes some other clergymen. Each society also has one or two themed and constant fancy dress elements, which are traditional, ranging from cavaliers and Zulu warriors to Native American chieftains and Siamese dancers.

SUSSEX CRAFTS

'A Sussex crook would be of no use to a Kent shepherd, and a man herding Dorset Horns would require still a different pattern.'

H.V. MORTON, *I SAW TWO ENGLANDS*, 1942

The raw materials and the nature of her landscape give Sussex her craft history and much of her ARCHITECTURAL HERITAGE, too. Today, when craft often means fancywork of a rather redundant function, it's interesting to look back on the old crafts and their cornerstone roles in the small country communities.

Six sorts of flintwork

FLINT BUILDING is still common in Sussex; the county is rich in the natural material and flintknapping – the chipping of flint to reveal the interior of the stone in flat or angled planes – is the oldest craft known there (there's plenty of evidence that it was practised to a high degree of skill in Neolithic times). Flint workers have a number of terms for different styles in flint building.

✣ **COBBLED** – unknapped pebbles laid in straight, even rows, or courses, to make a wall. The pebbles tend to lean in one or another direction – a slant left indicates a right-handed layer, and a slant to the right, a left-handed one.

✣ **COURSED** – knapped flints laid in courses, often interspersed with brick courses or decorative inset brick elements. Walls with a knapped flint surface facing outwards were known in Sussex dialect as 'snail-creep work'.

✣ **RANDOM-KNAPPED** – knapped flints used in random sizes, giving a characterful wall that needs careful laying.

✣ **RANDOM-SEMI-KNAPPED** – roughly knapped flints used in random sizes, resulting in a wall that looks instantly aged.

✣ **SQUARE-KNAPPED** – the most labour-intensive finish, consisting of flints knapped to an even-sized, flat-faced square. The flints can then be laid evenly in courses, like bricks.

✣ **GARRETTING** – the technique of fitting small pieces of flint into the mortar around the larger knapped flints. The resulting wall will show less mortar and have an overall more uniform look.

The Pyecombe crook

The SHEPHERDS' CROOKS forged at Pyecombe were famous for their quality; they had a larger curve at the top of iron, and a long angled tongue finished in a circle of the metal. The curve (the 'barrel') was to fit round the leg of a sheep; the tongue (the 'guide') was used as a persuader. Traditionally the crook refers only to the iron top part of the shepherd's staff.

Here is Richard Jefferies again, describing an encounter with a young shepherd on the Downs:

> *'His hook is not a Pycombe crook (for the best crooks used to be made at Pyecombe, a little Down hamlet), but he has another, which was made from a Pyecombe pattern. The village craftsman, whose shepherd's crooks were sought for all along the South Downs, is no more, and he has left no one able to carry on his work. He had an apprentice, but the apprentice has taken to another craft and cannot make crooks. The Pyecombe crook has a curve or semicircle, and then opens out straight; the straight part starts at a tangent from the semicircle. How difficult it is to describe so simple a matter as a shepherd's crook! In some way or other this Pyecombe form is found more effective for capturing sheep, but it is not so easy to make.'*

Pyecombe's village sign features a Pyecombe crook, and a crook is also used as a finial on the local church gate.

Sussex hedgers

The ARGOT OF HEDGELAYERS was so extremely local that it was said that men from different ends of the county did not understand each other if they met in the middle. In the list below, one definition leads to another:

- **ROSSEL** – in the Downs, a place in a wall low enough to step over; in the east Weald, a raddle (woven) fence; in the north and west of the county, a quick-layered hedge.
- **LAYERED HEDGE** – a quick hedge made by taking stakes from the old growth and weaving the rest between them, to make a solid structure. 'Layering' was interchangeable with 'splishering' or 'splashing' in different parts of Sussex.
- **SPLISHER** – could also mean to bury the cut ethers in the ground in the hope that they would take root to grow in the new hedge.

☛ *And so it goes on, every term ambiguous unless you were using it to someone from the same district or even village.*

SUSSEX SHEEP IN JAPAN

The skills of the Sussex shepherds and the quality of the wool produced by their sheep have long been admired, and Southdown wool is today in particular demand in Japan as filling for the traditional futons, thin mattresses used to sleep on. A futon filled with Southdown wool can cost (in yen) the equivalent of over a thousand pounds sterling.

SUSSEX CUSTOMS & TRADITIONS

'No Tea, but much Industrey and good Cheer.'

JAMES SPERSHOTT, *REMINISCENCES OF SUSSEX HOUSEHOLDS*, 1730s

Many of the county's CUSTOMS and TRADITIONS revolve around the FISHING and AGRICULTURE OF SUSSEX; each profession had its own specific superstitions, sayings and practices. Sussex being sheep country, it isn't surprising that a good many of these reflect the main events of the shepherd's year; the fisher fleets had their share of esoteric customs, too, and every profession or trade could boast at least a handful of traditions of its own.

A shepherd's counting rhyme

One-erum – *one*
Two-erum – *two*
Cock-erum – *three*
Shu-erum – *four*
Sith-erum – *five*
Sath-erum – *six*
Wineberry – *seven*
Wagtail – *eight*
Tarry diddle – *nine*
Den – *ten*

Shepherds in all counties have their own systems for counting, or 'telling' sheep into or out of a pasture, and this one is particularly recorded in and associated with Sussex. Usually the counting is done in pairs of sheep, so by the time the shepherd got to 'den', he would have counted twenty animals.

Five Sussex rituals

✣ BENDING IN DAY – a fisherman's picnic celebration, held on the beach at the beginning of the mackerel-fishing season. The crews' families were treated to food and drink around the boats on the shore. 'Bending in' is probably a corruption of 'benediction' – when a priest would bless the fishing fleet as it set out to sea.

✣ BLACK RAM NIGHT – an evening to mark the end of the shearing. The captain of each shearing team shared out the wages, and everyone repaired to the nearest inn, where they ate and drank, making their traditional toast:

If I had store,
By sheep and fold,
I'd give you gold.
But since I'm poor
By crook and bell,
I wish you well.

✣ **LONG ROPE DAY** (Good Friday) – a fisherman's skipping festival from Brighton. A long skipping rope was swung in the fish market, and each man skipped to the accompaniment of chanting and rhymes. This custom used to be more widespread, and at one point each boat or small group of boats had its own skipping rope. The custom is said to refer to the rope which hung Judas, and the ceremony is believed to bring good luck to the fleet.

✣ **HARVEST'S END** – a celebration for the end of a good harvest; at the close of the final day, the farmer gave each man who had worked in the fields a drink of beer (the 'hollering pot'), and the workers joined in a circle and sang:

We've ploughed, we've sowed,
We've reaped, we've mowed,
We've carried the last load
And never o'er throwed.
Hip, hip, hurrah!

✣ **LIFTING** – another shepherds' ritual, practised at weddings, in which the bride and bridegroom were raised on decorated hurdles, seated on sheepskins, and carried triumphantly round the shepherd's flock.

A smith's celebration

Given Sussex's great love of FIREWORKS and EXPLOSIONS, the particular tendency of her smiths to 'fire the anvil' to mark a celebration is not surprising. Firing the anvil is the creation of an explosion in the hollow heart of the anvil – using gunpowder, a bung and a wick, it is converted into a makeshift cannon, and can create a sizeable report. First the hole in the base of the anvil is filled with gunpowder, then bunged with a wooden stopper. A narrow hole is bored through the stopper and a fuse pushed through it, then lit.

Dangerous? Yes. Noisy? Yes. Traditional? Definitely – there are records of this practice reaching back to the eighteenth century and beyond, for weddings, to celebrate national holidays and occasions, to mark a victory at election time, and, of course, on 23 November, St Clement's Day. St Clement is the patron saint of blacksmiths.

SPOILING THE SHIP

At shearing time, bands of itinerant shearers went from farm to farm and each band had a 'tar boy', whose job it was to dab tar on any accidental cuts to the sheep. The saying 'spoiling the ship for a ha'porth of tar', which is often assumed to have naval origins, actually comes from this practice – 'ship' being the dialect pronunciation of 'sheep'.

GAMES & SPORTS

'Traditional pub games are dying out... but Sussex is still the heartland of dwyle flunking and toad-in-the-hole.'

THE SUSSEX *ARGUS*, 2002

Rich in INDIGENOUS SPORT, Sussex, along with Kent, is credited for being the cradle of ENGLISH CRICKET. Many less orthodox games were and are played here, for the county is home to the only known league for the game of 'toad', for example, in which brass discs are thrown at a chair-shaped 'board', with a hold in the centre of the seat, as well as hosting the WORLD MARBLE CHAMPIONSHIPS. Whatever your game, you are likely to find a Sussex team for it.

Marbles season

MARBLES have been found in England dating back to Roman times, and Sussex has many traditions based around the game. Marbles 'season' falls between Ash Wednesday and Good Friday; historically, to play beyond midday on the Friday was unlucky. The Greyhound Inn at Tinsley Green, in West Sussex, has hosted the World Marble Championships since 1932, and today over 20 teams and 100 players battle it out for the title over several days.

The classic game sounds deceptively simple: 49 marbles are placed in a cement ring six feet across, and each player 'shoots' them with their tolley, or shooting marble, winning a point for each marble knocked out of the ring. The first to reach 25 points wins the game. It's much harder than it sounds.

Marble terminology

✣ **TOLLEY OR TAW** – the 'shooting' marble; must not be smaller than half-an-inch or larger than three-quarters of an inch in diameter.

✣ **MIB OR KIMMIE** – a marble that is 'shot'; must not be larger than five-eighths of an inch in diameter.

✣ **NOSE DROP** – deciding the order in which the players go: each player drops their tolley from their nose-height onto a line drawn in the sand. The tolley that lands nearest the line starts the game.

✣ **LAGGING** – an alternative way to start the game – the marble is rolled towards the 'lag', or start line, rather than dropped.

✣ **FLICKING** – the move by which a tolley is flicked from the player's hand.

✣ **KNUCKLING DOWN** – the rule that says one knuckle must be touching the ground whilst flicking

The home of British cricket

The village of ROBERTSBRIDGE is a very English home for the quintessential English game, and is so-called because it has been the production centre for GRAY-NICOLLS, one of the foremost makers of cricket bats, since 1876. They claim to be the only company to grow all their own willow.

Preliminaries to making the perfect cricket bat:

- Use a willow tree around 15 years old and 40ft tall – any older and the wood is no longer flexible enough.
- Measured from 5ft up from the ground, the 10ft of central trunk should be free of branches and about 4ft in circumference.
- This central section is cut into four pieces, 'cuts', 2ft 4in long.
- Cut 6 'clefts', the raw form of a cricket bat, from each piece.
- Season in a temperature-regulated kiln for six weeks.
- Press each cleft with a weight of 2,000lbs per square inch, to make it tough and durable.

The earliest team

On 17 June 1836 the Sussex Cricket Fund was set up in Brighton to support county matches, and three years later it was formalised into the SUSSEX COUNTY CRICKET CLUB – the first in England. It played first against the Marylebone Cricket Club on 10 and 11 June, 1839.

The milkmaid's game

The odd name for STOOLBALL, a forerunner of cricket and rounders that originated in Sussex and is recorded as far back as the 1500s, is said to have come from the milkmaids who were the earliest players and who, allegedly, used their milking stools to mark the wicket. It is still mainly, although not exclusively, a game for women. The rules and terminology are broadly similar to those of cricket, with runs, catches, and boundaries, but with eight rather than six balls in each over. Stoolball is played with underarm bowling. Unusually, though, the bat is paddle-shaped and is made of willow.

Length of pitch . . . . **16 yards**
Diameter of boundary: . . . . . **90 yards**
Bowling crease: . . . . **10 yards**
from the batsman's wicket
Team size: . . . . **11 players**

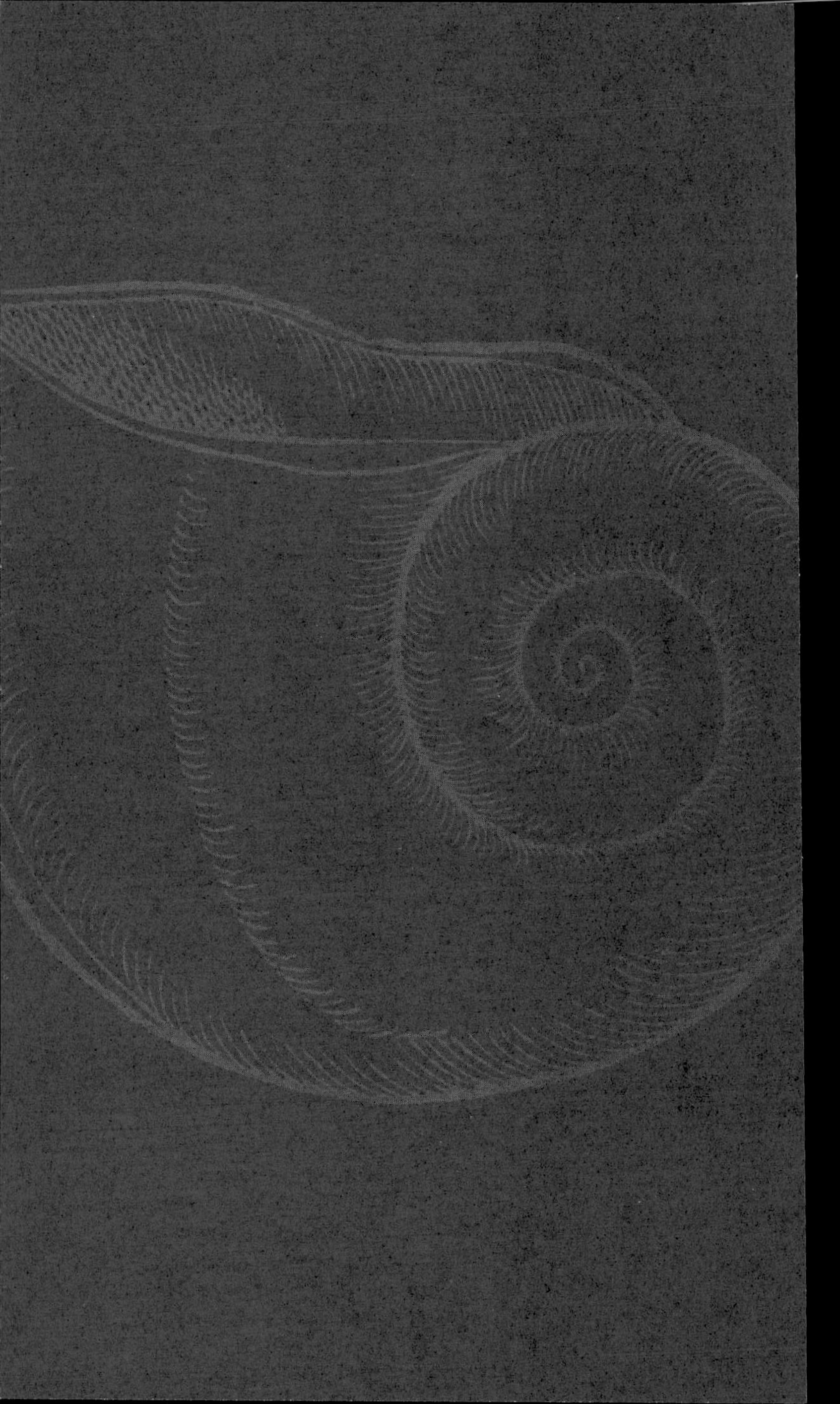

FURTHER READING & INDEX

FURTHER READING

There is a vast range of books on Sussex available, both general and topic-specific. This list suggests some of the most appealing – some in print, some (sadly) long out of it. All are enjoyable reading, but you may have to do a little detective work to track down some of the older and more obscure titles.

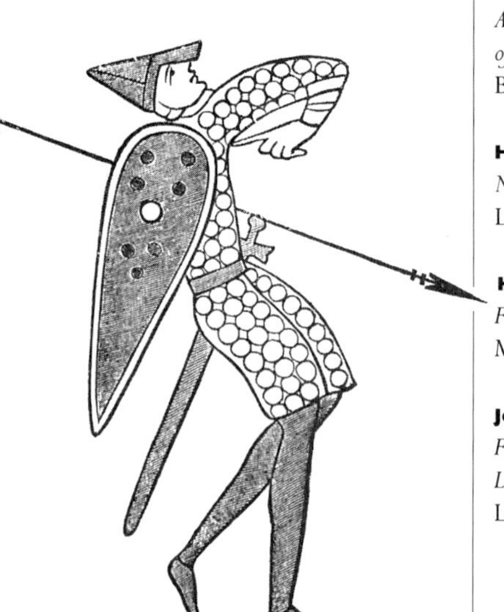

Armstrong, J.R.
A History of Sussex
Phillimore & Co. Ltd, 1961

Arscott, D.
Curiosities of East Sussex
S.B. Publications, 1991

Arscott, D.
Curiosities of West Sussex
S.B. Publications, 1993

Arthur, D.
A Sussex Life: The Memories of Gilbert Sargent, Countryman
Barrie & Jenkins Ltd., 1989

Hudson, W. H.
Nature in Downland
Longman, Green & Co., 1900

Hutchinson, G.
Fuller of Sussex, a Georgian Squire
M. & W. Morgan, 1993

Jefferies, R.
Field & Hedgerow: Being the Last Essays of Richard Jefferies
Longmans, Green, 1897

Jefferies, R., ed. S.J. Looker
Jefferies' Countryside
Constable, 1944

Lucas, E. V.
Highways & Byways of Sussex
Macmillan & Co., 1904

Nairn, I., & Pevsner, N.
The Buildings of England: Sussex
Penguin Books, 1965

Parish, Rev. W. D.
Dictionary of the Sussex Dialect
Farncombe & Co., 1875

Parish, Rev. W.D. & Hall, H.
Dictionary of the Sussex Dialect (extended)
R.J. Ackford, 1957

Russell, M.
Prehistoric Sussex
S.B. Publications, 2002

Simpson, J.
The Folklore of Sussex
B.T. Batsford Ltd., 1973

Swinfen, W. & Arscott, D.
Hidden Sussex
BBC Radio Sussex, 1984

Wales, T.
Sussex as She Wus Spoke: A Guide to the Sussex Dialect
S.B. Publications, 2000

Willard, B.
Sussex
B.T. Batsford, 1965

Wills, B.
Bypaths in Downland
Methuen, 1927

Wills, B.
The Downland Shepherds
Alan Sutton, 1989

If you're in search of Sussex fiction, Stella Gibbons' *Cold Comfort Farm*, any of the Mapp and Lucia novels by E.F. Benson, or Kipling's Sussex writings, in particular *Puck of Pook's Hill* and *Rewards and Fairies*, are all easily available and well worth a visit.

INDEX

Alfriston *11, 27, 37, 65*
Amberley *43, 59, 69*
anchorites *52-3*
artists/sculptors *35, 50, 53, 76-7*
Arundel *10, 28, 42-3, 59, 62*
Ashdown Forest *21, 31*

Balcombe *54, 55*
battles *44-5*
Beachy Head *17, 27, 71*
bees *18, 32, 67*
Bevis of Hampton *28-9*
Bexhill *11, 32*
birds *20-1, 33, 36, 59, 66-7*
Blackboys, ghosts *27*
blacksmiths *87*
Bloomsbury Group *46, 70, 73*
Bodiam castle *42, 43*
Bognor Regis *78, 79*
Bonfire Night *25, 38, 82-3*
Bramber *43, 51, 71*
Brede, ogre *29*
Brighton *11*
  buildings *15, 51, 81*
  Chattri *49*
  cricket *89*
  Phoebe Hessel *45*
  piers *78-9*
  pubs *65*
  railway *54*
  spa town *62, 63, 78*
  witchcraft *31*
  writers/artists *75, 77*
Brighton Rock *17*
Burwash *23, 46, 48, 75*

Castles *27, 42-3*
cats *21, 70, 71*
cattle *23, 37, 66, 67*
Chanctonbury Ring *33*
Chichester *11, 37, 52, 53, 59, 80*
chickens *37, 66-7*
Chiddingly, Farley Farm *50*
chillie *47*
churches *34, 36-7, 45, 48, 49, 52-3*
cinque ports *16*
Civil War *41, 43, 44*
coastline *16-17, 71, 78-9*
coats of arms *10*
Crawley *11, 29*
cricket *89*
Cuckfield *15, 32*
cuckoos *33*
customs/traditions *12, 32, 86-7*

Devil's Dyke *37*
dialect *19, 34-5, 57, 58, 85, 87, 93*
Ditchling *12, 27, 31, 52, 62*
dogs *27, 70, 71*
dragons *26-7, 36*
drink *58, 62-3, 64-5*

East Grinstead *11, 39, 51, 64*
Eastbourne *11, 12, 14, 55, 78-9*

Fairies *32*
farming *66-7, 69, 70, 85, 86, 87*
fauna *12, 19, 20-1, 33, 67, 70-1, 85*
Firle *46, 50, 70*
fish/seafood *17, 59, 60, 61, 79, 86, 87*
Fishbourne Roman villa *47, 61, 69*
flint buildings *51, 53, 84*
flora *12, 18-19, 47*
Folkington *52, 74*
follies *34, 49, 80-1*
food *33, 57, 58-61, 66-7, 74*
fossils *14-15*
Fuller, 'Mad' Jack *34, 80, 92*

Gardens/gardening *46-7, 51*
ghosts *27, 42, 65*
giants *28-9*
Goring-by-Sea *53, 75*
gravestones *34, 48-9, 69, 74, 75*
Great Dixter, Northiam *47*

Hardham anchorite *52-3*
Hassocks, Newtimber Place *50*
Hastings *11, 16*
  Aleister Crowley *30*
  battle of *44, 45*
  castle *27, 43*
  fossils *14*
  Lizzie Siddal *77*
  pier/net shops *78, 79*
  Rarities *20-1*
  sculpture *77*
Haywards Heath *44, 54, 63, 65*
Heathfield *11, 22, 48, 81*
hedging *85*
Henfield *27, 32*
Herstmonceux *43, 48, 51*
Hessel, Phoebe *45*
Horsham *11, 15, 22, 51, 64, 65*
Horsted Keynes *49*
houses *14-15, 50-1, 84*
hunting *69, 70*

Inns and pubs *27, 43, 60, 64-5, 88*

Jefferies, Richard *9, 75, 85, 92, 93*

Kipling, Rudyard *9, 32, 46, 55, 73, 74-5, 93*

Leonardslee Gardens *21*
Lewes *11*
  battle of *44*
  Bonfire Night *25, 38, 82-3*
  bricks *51*
  castle *43*
  churches *53*
  fossils *15*
  martyrs *25, 38-9, 83*
  sculpture *76, 77*
  White Hart Inn *58, 60*
Lullington *52, 53*

Marbles *73, 88*
martyrs *25, 38-9, 83*
Michelham Priory *23, 27, 69*
mills *23, 69*
monsters *26-7, 29*
monuments *34, 38-9, 48-9*
murderer, acid bath *29*
museums *20, 38, 43, 51, 69, 71*

Parish, William *11, 19, 34-5, 93*
Patcham *49, 52*
pets *70-1*
Petworth *23, 50-1, 63, 81*
Pevensey Castle *27, 43*

Piddinghoe *11, 52, 53*
piers *78-9*
Piltdown Man *15*
place names *11, 32*
ponds *22-3, 26*
puddings *58, 59, 61*
Pulborough *11, 51, 59, 63*
Pyecombe crook *85*

Railways *54-5, 74*
Ringmer, tortoise *71*
rivers *22, 23*
Robertsbridge *69, 89*
Rodmell, Monks House *46-7, 49, 70*
Romans *47, 60, 61, 69, 88*
Rye *16, 22, 43, 46, 59, 65*

Saints *25, 36-7*
Saxons *11, 13, 45, 66*
shepherds/sheep *23, 66, 85, 86-7, 93*
Shoreham *22, 61*
Singleton *23, 51, 69*
smuggling *16-17*
snakes *25, 26-7, 36*
society *12, 57, 68-9*
soldiers *44, 45, 49*
South Downs Way *12*
St Leonard's Forest *22, 25, 26-7, 36*
statistics *10-13*
Steyning *36-7, 53, 62, 67*
stoolball *73, 89*
superstitions *19, 32-3, 52*

Trugs *47*

Vineyards *63*

Wakehurst Place *18*
Weald and Downland Open Air Museum *23, 51, 69*
West Dean *35, 47*
wife-selling *65*
Wilmington *27, 29*
witchcraft *19, 30-1*
Woolf, Leonard and Virginia *46-7, 49, 70, 73*
Worthing *11, 78, 79*
writers/poets *9, 21, 27, 31, 46, 49, 62-3, 68, 74-5, 77, 79, 93*